Photo by Stan Barouh

Gretchen Cleevely and Bill Kux in a scene from the Arena Stage production of *Dimly*

DIMLY PERCEIVED THREATS TO THE SYSTEM

BY JON KLEIN

★

★

DRAMATISTS
PLAY SERVICE
INC.

DIMLY PERCEIVED THREATS TO THE SYSTEM was workshopped and developed at New York Stage and Film and at Carnegie-Mellon's Showcase for New Plays in the summer of 1996.

DIMLY PERCEIVED THREATS TO THE SYSTEM was first produced by Illusion Theater, Minneapolis, Minnesota; Michael Robins and Bonnie Morris, Producing Directors.

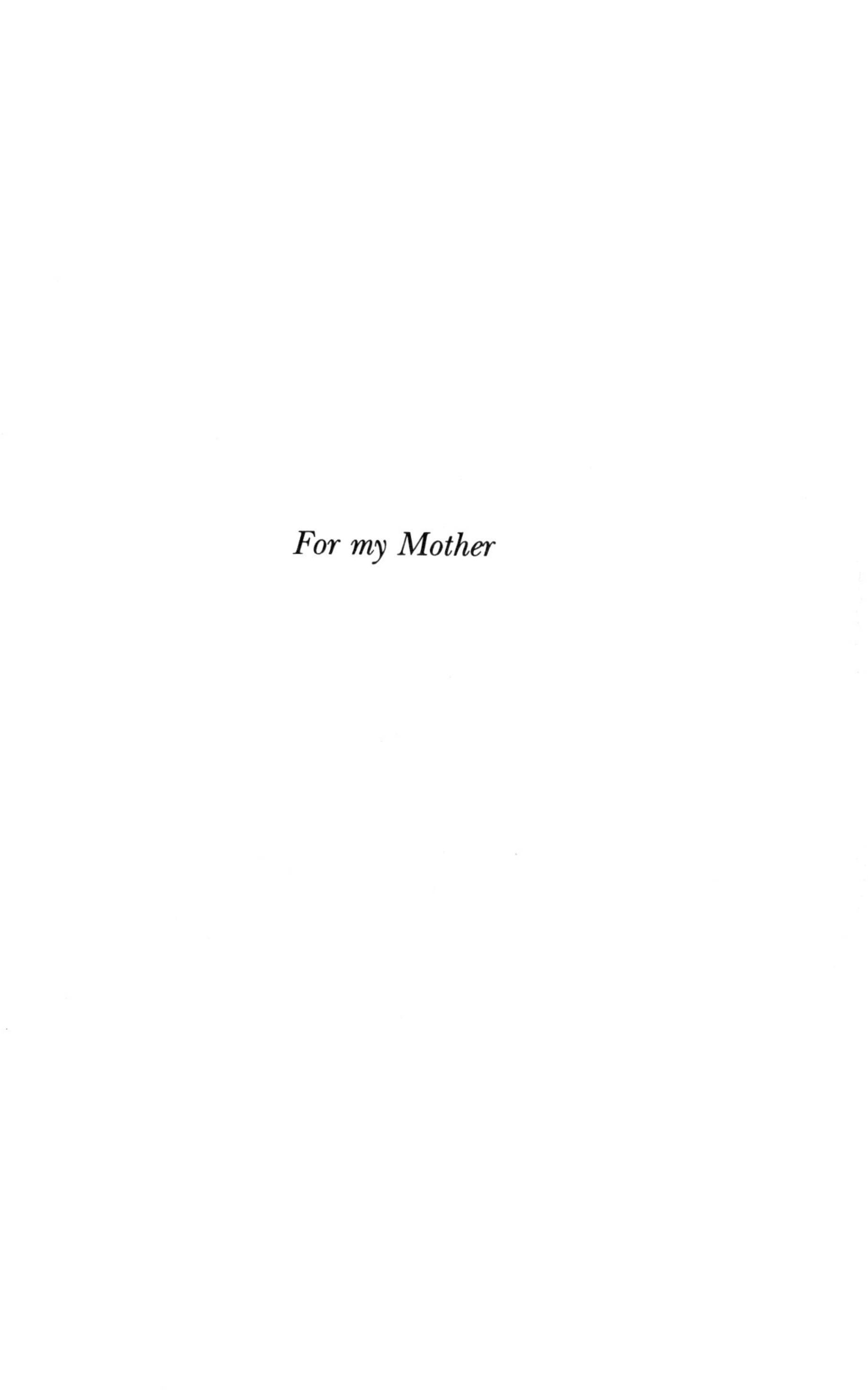

For my Mother

DIMLY PERCEIVED THREATS TO THE SYSTEM was produced by Arena Stage (Douglas C. Wager, Artistic Director) in Washington, D.C., in January, 1998. It was directed by Douglas C. Wager; the set design was by Tony Cisek; the costume design was by Barbra Kravitz; the lighting design was by Nancy Schertler; the sound design was by Susan R. White; the dramaturg was Kenneth J. Cernigua; and the stage manager was Amy L. Vining. The cast was as follows:

MARLYS HAUSER . . . . Jacalyn O'Shaughnessy
JOSH HAUSER. . . . . Terrence Caza
CHRISTINE HAUSER. . . . . Gretchen Cleevely
MR. SYKES . . . . Bill Kux
MEGAN LONE . . . . Holly Twyford
DR. GREY. . . . . Brigid Cleary

DIMLY PERCEIVED THREATS TO THE SYSTEM was produced by Illusion Theater (Michael H. Robins and Bonnie Morris, Producing Directors), in Minneapolis, Minnesota, in November, 1996. It was directed by Kent Stephens; the set design was by Dean Holzman; the lighting design was by Darren McCroom; the costume design was by Jeanne Mallet; the visual image design was by Kristin Reed; the sound design was by Randall E. Seitz; the production stage manager was Karen Gundlach. The cast was as follows:

MARLYS HAUSER . . . . Beth Gilleland
JOSH HAUSER . . . . Chris Denton
CHRISTINE HAUSER . . . . Victoria Engelmayer
MR. SYKES. . . . . Peter Schmitz
MEGAN LONE. . . . . Gail Hammerschmidt Quinn
DR. GREY. . . . . Mary McDevitt

DIMLY PERCEIVED THREATS TO THE SYSTEM was originally presented in staged readings by New York Stage and Film, at Vassar College, and at Carnegie Mellon's Showcase for New Plays in Pittsburgh, Pennsylvania, in June, 1996.

CHARACTERS

(2 men, 4 women)

In order of appearance:

MARLYS HAUSER (pronounced Már–liss) — a consultant

JOSH — her husband, a documentary film maker

CHRISTINE — 13, their daughter

MR. SYKES — a school therapist

MEGAN LONE — a television producer

DR. GREY — a general practitioner

Scene Titles are taken from entries in sociological dictionaries. Their use in any production of the play is entirely optional.

DIMLY PERCEIVED THREATS TO THE SYSTEM

ACT ONE

Achievement Motivation

Marlys, at a podium.

MARLYS. They want you to be afraid. It's in the corporate interest. Just take a look at the very language they use to keep you in line. "Downsizing." "Scaling back." "Recession." "Work reduction." Deliberately designed to make you feel small. Insignificant. (*Pause.*) Remember when you *were* small? It's not that long ago. I look around this hall and see children playing with bubbles in the back yard. There's a design team in the making. Or running around the house in homemade capes, pretending to be Superman or Wonder Woman. Perfecting management techniques at the age of five. Or maybe having tea and biscuits with imaginary friends. Which is pretty much any sales conference, don't you think? They say a kid's job is to play. Does your job feel like play? Maybe it should. *(Appreciative chuckling from the front.)* And when you played, and you scraped your knee or cut your finger, you ran to your mom and she kissed it and made it better. So who do you run to when *you* have a boo-boo? When the numbers don't crunch. Or you lose that crucial account. Who's gonna kiss *your* mistake and make it better? The office manager? The executive vice-president? Not likely. Instead they'll tell you to stand in the corner. Oh, it may take the form of a performance review, but the effect is the same. To make you feel like a naughty child. A corporation should be like an expanded family — so why won't this one let you grow up? *(Low murmuring from the front.)* You do your best at home. Don't you? You make sure the kids are clothed and eat healthy meals. You listen to your spouse and offer understanding. You somehow manage to keep the family together. So why don't these methods work in the corporate world? And if a corporation is like a family, you can only imagine the emotional effect of a massive layoff. *(Startled voices from the crowd.)* Now calm down. It won't affect all of you. Just 1500 or so. *(The voices rise to the level of an angry mob.)* You may feel like an unwanted child. But there's always adoption. Someone else out there will love you. *(The voices reach a crescendo.)* Have I said too much? *(She looks around and behind her.)* Is there a back exit? *(Marlys is trapped in place. The mob noise builds to a crescendo, then lights and sound suddenly go out.)*

Methodological Individualism

Josh at the breakfast table, drinking coffee and reading a newspaper. Christine enters, carrying a backpack and drinking a cola.

CHRISTINE. What's with Mom?
JOSH. She had a bad day at work yesterday.
CHRISTINE. What happened?
JOSH. I'm not sure. But apparently it affected the Nasdaq index. *(He looks up at his daughter.)* What's that?
CHRISTINE. What?
JOSH. That outfit.
CHRISTINE. What?
JOSH. That thing you're wearing.
CHRISTINE. What about it?

JOSH. What's it supposed to be? *(Christine calls off.)*
CHRISTINE. Mom!
JOSH. I mean really, Christine, what's the message you're delivering here?
CHRISTINE. Mom!
JOSH. Don't call your mother. I'm your father, and I have the right to ask these questions.
CHRISTINE. Mom!
JOSH. It's not a personal criticism. I just want to know your intentions.
CHRISTINE. Intentions?
JOSH. Why do you want to look like that?
CHRISTINE. What's wrong with it?
JOSH. It doesn't suit you. It doesn't reflect your personality.
CHRISTINE. How would you know?
JOSH. I think I know my own daughter.
CHRISTINE. Since when?
JOSH. Don't be smart.
CHRISTINE. You think I'm stupid.
JOSH. Of course not. Although I think you could use a little more thought in your choice of attire.
CHRISTINE. My clothes are stupid.
JOSH. Yes, I'd say so.
CHRISTINE. Mom!
JOSH. Do you know how insulting that is?
CHRISTINE. What?
JOSH. Calling her to take your side. I'm still your father, like it or not. I have a valuable function here.
CHRISTINE. I don't need this shit.
JOSH. Of course you don't *need* it. Nobody *needs* it. That's why I'm *offering* it to you, in the form of constructive criticism. All I ask is that you have enough respect to establish a dialogue with me. Just meet me halfway, Christine. Can you do that? *(Pause.)*
CHRISTINE. I guess.
JOSH. Good. Now go change your clothes.
CHRISTINE. Mom! *(Marlys enters.)*
MARLYS. What.
CHRISTINE. Tell Dad to stop.

MARLYS. Stop it, Josh.
JOSH. You don't even know what's going on.
MARLYS. What's going on?
CHRISTINE. Dad's bugging me.
MARLYS. Stop bugging her, Josh.
JOSH. What about that outfit?
MARLYS. What about it?
JOSH. You don't have a problem with that?
CHRISTINE. *Mom ...*
MARLYS. It's her body, Josh.
JOSH. Not until she's eighteen. Until then I'm the one feeding it and educating it.
MARLYS. She's been dressing herself for a while now.
CHRISTINE. Yeah. I can even tie my own shoes.
JOSH. I told you once, don't get smart. *(To Marlys.)* I'm just asking her what in the hell she's trying to express. How do people *perceive* her?
MARLYS. She's thirteen, Josh. She's trying to figure out who she is. Clothes are a part of the process. I'm sure you offended plenty of people when you were her age.
JOSH. Sure I did. That was the *point.* All our fringe jackets, peace buttons and long hair served to give a message to society.
CHRISTINE. What's the message of bell-bottoms?
JOSH. We were proclaiming a social revolution. From our platform shoes all the way up to our headbands. We were saying, screw you and your colonial wars, screw you and your ghetto building, screw you and your military-industrial profit making. It made a statement.
MARLYS. And that statement was "screw you"?
JOSH. So to speak.
CHRISTINE. How come you get to talk like that and I don't?
JOSH. You can say or do anything you want, as long as it makes a viable point about the social system. Never let it be said that I stifled my kid's creativity.
CHRISTINE. Can I get pierced?
JOSH. Absolutely not.
CHRISTINE. *Mom ...*
MARLYS. Eat your breakfast, Christine.

CHRISTINE. I don't want any.

MARLYS. You need more than a Coke for breakfast.

CHRISTINE. I'll be late.

MARLYS. I don't care what you eat at school, at home in the morning you're going to eat something with a little nutritional value. Have some cereal.

CHRISTINE. *Dad ...*

JOSH. It's all right, Christine.

MARLYS. Don't contradict me in front of her.

JOSH. She doesn't need it, Marlys. Maybe Norman Rockwell's kids had scrambled eggs and pancakes, but kids today are on a different schedule. Trust me, she'll survive without raisin bran.

MARLYS. I don't agree.

CHRISTINE. *Dad ...*

JOSH. It's all right, honey. Go to school.

CHRISTINE. Thank you.

JOSH. After you change your clothes.

CHRISTINE. *Mom ...*

MARLYS. Just get the hell out of here, will you? *(Pause. Christine angrily throws her empty cola can on the floor and storms out.)*

JOSH. That was helpful.

MARLYS. That's what I get paid for. To be helpful.

JOSH. Just because you screwed things up yesterday —

MARLYS. Christine's not here, Josh. You can say it now. I fucked up. Not screwed up. Fucked up.

JOSH. There's no talking to you when you're like this.

MARLYS. Maybe that will be my lecture for today — "Fuck Up With Impunity." I like it.

JOSH. Do you like unemployment?

MARLYS. See, you'd probably take that as a sign of failure. Like if your little film project was cancelled.

JOSH. My "little" project?

MARLYS. Okay, your momentous, ground-breaking, earth-shaking project. What if it got canned? You'd be devastated.

JOSH. Chances are I'd have a bit of a mood swing, yes.

MARLYS. See? That's what I'm saying about our value systems. Work isn't that important to me.

JOSH. Is that so? You think you could handle it.

MARLYS. What, joblessness?
JOSH. That's right.
MARLYS. Yes, I think so. It would be a blow to my ego, of course, but I don't think I'd be completely destroyed.
JOSH. I'm relieved to hear it.
MARLYS. Relieved?
JOSH. Definitely. It makes this decision a little easier for me. And Christine too.
MARLYS. What decision?
JOSH. I wish there was a more comfortable way to announce these things ...
MARLYS. Spit it out, Josh. What are you talking about?
JOSH. All right. We've decided to let you go. *(Pause.)*
MARLYS. What?
JOSH. Look, Mrs. Hauser. You're obviously not thrilled with your function here. And let's face it, you're affecting the general morale. Now ordinarily, we'd try to find you a more suitable position, some role that would provide you with more satisfaction. But there's just no room for lateral movement. Wife and mother are the only openings at this point in time. So Christine and I had a little conference, and we decided it would be best — for all concerned — to terminate.
MARLYS. You're joking, right?
JOSH. I wish I were.
MARLYS. You're *firing* me?
JOSH. We'll offer a generous severance, of course. And enthusiastic recommendations. I'm sure Christine would be happy to mention your driving skills.
MARLYS. You can't just dismiss me. I gave *birth* to that child!
JOSH. A little late to ask for workers' compensation.
MARLYS. But you *need* me.
JOSH. Oh, don't worry about us. We've got some very qualified candidates coming over for interviews this evening. One of them even *bakes*. So it's probably best if you clear out your drawers sometime today.
MARLYS. That's it? After all these years?
JOSH. Out of my hands.
MARLYS. If it's just an attitude problem, I can adjust.

JOSH. Well, I don't know. We want to be fair, of course.

MARLYS. See? I'm smiling already. I can be incredibly cheery if I put my mind to it. How about a bag lunch? I can whip up deviled ham in three minutes flat.

JOSH. Perhaps we *have* been hasty ...

MARLYS. There's more I can do around the house. I'll give it extra effort.

JOSH. Weekends too?

MARLYS. You got it.

JOSH. Well. I suppose we could try a probationary period, see how things go.

MARLYS. Oh, thank you, sir! Thank you, thank you! *(She grabs his hand and pumps it like a well handle.)*

JOSH. What are you doing?

MARLYS. I won't let you down, I promise.

JOSH. Marlys!

MARLYS. Yes! Call me Marlys! That's a good sign!

JOSH. Let go of me! *(She withdraws her hand, disoriented.)* What's wrong with you?

MARLYS. Nothing. Sorry. What were we talking about?

JOSH. Our value systems. And how different they are.

MARLYS. Not at all. They're exactly the same. Work is the priority. Work, family, success. Right?

JOSH. I guess so.

MARLYS. Let me just say that I'm very, very happy to be here. *(He looks at her strangely.)*

JOSH. Well ... good. I'm happy if you're happy.

MARLYS. I can make you lunch.

JOSH. No thanks, I'm running late. I'll go to the diner as usual.

MARLYS. How about a pie?

JOSH. You don't have time for that.

MARLYS. Oh yes I do. I've got the time. I'll *make* the fucking time.

JOSH. Just ... go to the bakery.

MARLYS. All right.

JOSH. And try to relax, will you? Or the next thing you know ... you'll be out of a job. *(He kisses her good-bye and exits.)*

MARLYS. Just *try* it, you bastard.

Cognitive Dissonance

Josh and Megan at a film editing machine. Josh holds a script in his lap.

JOSH. Now here's the sequence. Lots of backyard barbecues, Ward Cleaver types with pipes and "kiss the cook" aprons. Fashionable housewives with high heels, stretch pants and cigarettes, pushing their kids on swing sets. Rec room limbo contests, martini pitchers scattered around like religious icons. Ramsey Lewis and Ella Fitzgerald on the phonograph, lots of snapping fingers, children wearing sunglasses at night, everything's cool. Huge station wagons unloading kids in front of suburban schools like the carriers at Normandy. All very fifties. Republican wet dreamland. I'll do the voiceover. *(He starts the film rolling. Megan watches the screen as he reads.)* "The nineties represent a constant conflict between two value systems. That of the baby boomers, desperately trying to maintain their own nostalgia for the post-war era. And that of their children, who can't imagine a life without personal stress and economic uncertainty. No wonder the late Kurt Cobain, lead singer for Nirvana, proclaimed *Mayberry R.F.D.* as his favorite TV show." *(She stops the reels.)*

JOSH. Wait, there's more.

MEGAN. Let's slow down and assess, Josh. I'm wondering about the emphasis.

JOSH. Go on.

MEGAN. Well, it's pretty exclusionary, don't you think?

JOSH. What do you mean?

MEGAN. All this focus on the nuclear family. Not everyone can relate, you know?

JOSH. That's the point. I'm showing how obsolete the old systems are.

MEGAN. Without showing us any *new* systems. There's not enough time spent on alternative lifestyles. Some people might feel excluded.

JOSH. People like who?

MEGAN. Well ... people like me. *(Pause.)*

JOSH. Like you?

MEGAN. Don't think about me.

JOSH. What ... what did you say?

MEGAN. People like me. Who aren't married.

JOSH. Didn't you just ...

MEGAN. What?

JOSH. Nothing. Go on.

MEGAN. What I'm saying is, I don't have this nostalgia for an old-fashioned family life that you claim is so common. I don't even know what it means to have a real family. And I don't really miss it.

JOSH. But without a family, what do you do for emotional fulfillment?

MEGAN. You're thinking about me.

JOSH. What?

MEGAN. A cat. I have a cat.

JOSH. What about a cat?

MEGAN. I don't like repeating myself, Josh.

JOSH. I'm sorry.

MEGAN. I was just saying that my cat provides all the emotional fulfillment I need.

JOSH. Oh.

MEGAN. Give her a string and some catnip, and little Evita gives me all the unconditional love I'll ever ask for. Far more than I could ever ask from any human being.

JOSH. So when you mention alternate lifestyles —

MEGAN. Adulterous.

JOSH. What ... did you say?

MEGAN. You heard me. Alternative. Not alternate. There's a difference.

JOSH. Of course.

MEGAN. There's adoption, unmarried parents, single parents, same-sex parents, childless families, communal groups — the list goes on and on.

JOSH. But that's my point exactly. What really defines a family today? The traditional nuclear family is being threatened by new definitions.

MEGAN. Well, if you feel that way — I'd love to see you.

JOSH. Say that again?

MEGAN. I said I'd love to see more evidence. Am I speaking too softly?

JOSH. Maybe ... just a little.

MEGAN. You're too young for a hearing aid, Josh. Do you think you could provide some more lifestyle comparisons? That would please the grant givers. And God knows, this film won't get made without them.

JOSH. I could do that.

MEGAN. Good. Let's take a break. You're having trouble concentrating. Want some coffee?

JOSH. That would be ... helpful. *(Megan reaches for a nearby thermos and pours coffee into a paper cup.)* I have to confess something to you.

MEGAN. Definitely time for a break. Let's hear it.

JOSH. When you brought up alternative lifestyles, I thought you meant ... that you were ... you yourself were ...

MEGAN. Gay?

JOSH. I don't mean to embarrass you.

MEGAN. Not at all. After all — you're right. At least ... most recently.

JOSH. Oh. I see.

MEGAN. Don't think about me.

JOSH. I'm not.

MEGAN. You're not what, gay? Everyone's aware of that, Josh. Don't get threatened.

JOSH. Sorry. Go on.

MEGAN. See, I'm not exclusive to either gender. I'm bisexual.

JOSH. How does that work exactly?

MEGAN. What, you want the sequence? Let's see. Man, man, woman, man, woman, woman, man, woman, woman. It's all rather algebraic.

JOSH. I didn't mean —

MEGAN. Although I did leave out a few extended periods of masturbation.

JOSH. And thank you for that.

MEGAN. I wish you wouldn't look at me like that.

JOSH. Umm ... There's a little more on this reel.
MEGAN. Don't pretend you didn't hear me.
JOSH. Sorry. I wasn't sure ...
MEGAN. See? This is why I don't like discussing it. You're defining me according to my sexual preferences. Rather than as who I am.
JOSH. No I'm not.
MEGAN. I can see it in your face. Don't try to hide it. You perceive me as a different person now.
JOSH. No I don't.
MEGAN. You think I'm confused. I can assure you I'm not.
JOSH. Look, you've got me all wrong.
MEGAN. Fine. Let's move on. How do you explain your massive erection?
JOSH. What?
MEGAN. The last election. How do you explain the results of the last election, in light of these family value issues?
JOSH. I'm not ... sure.
MEGAN. You don't look well, Josh.
JOSH. I guess I'm ... preoccupied.
MEGAN. Work is the answer. Shall we get down to it? *(Pause.)*
JOSH. Meaning?

Measures of Central Tendency

Mr. Sykes at his desk. Christine sits opposite.

MR. SYKES. What happened, Christine? *(Pause. Christine doesn't look at him.)* Did somebody say something? *(Pause.)* Was there a disagreement? *(Pause.)* You know we're just going to sit here until we get to the bottom of this. *(Pause.)* Do you have something against someone? *(Pause.)* Do you have something against food?
CHRISTINE. Bologna.

MR. SYKES. I'm sorry you think so.
CHRISTINE. No, I mean ... bologna sandwiches.
MR. SYKES. I see.
CHRISTINE. I don't like them.
MR. SYKES. So you spit on their food.
CHRISTINE. It's disgusting. Made out of pig guts and ears and shit. They grind them up and add food coloring.
MR. SYKES. I see you're an expert on the subject.
CHRISTINE. It shouldn't be allowed.
MR. SYKES. You think bologna should be outlawed.
CHRISTINE. Yeah.
MR. SYKES. So it was your self-appointed duty to expectorate on the lunches of three classmates.
CHRISTINE. I was surrounded. I had to do something.
MR. SYKES. Those three students come from poor families, Christine. They eat bologna because bologna is cheap. Not because they're insensitive to the dignity of barnyard animals.
CHRISTINE. There are other things they could eat.
MR. SYKES. Not when a family is stretching a budget. So I suggest you leave your saliva to yourself.
CHRISTINE. Yes sir.
MR. SYKES. Are you sure there's not something else going on? Like at home?
CHRISTINE. Not that I can think of. My father beats me while my mother watches. But that's completely normal. Isn't it?
MR. SYKES. That's not funny, Christine.
CHRISTINE. So don't laugh.
MR. SYKES. The very fact that you choose to joke about such things would lead people to speculate about it.
CHRISTINE. All right. I take it back.
MR. SYKES. Are you angry at your parents?
CHRISTINE. Why should I be angry? They love me so much. They tell me what to eat, what to wear, what to say, what to think, what to do. They would rather sacrifice their own needs to make sure I'm happy.
MR. SYKES. This is what they tell you, obviously.
CHRISTINE. All the time.

MR. SYKES. There are many kinds of love, Christine. But it's not always easy to figure out. I'm three times your age, and I haven't figured it out yet. I've got an ex-wife and a kid who doesn't even get to live with me. What kind of love is that? Some of us just aren't very good at it.

CHRISTINE. So what?

MR. SYKES. You're right. Not your problem. Let me ask you this, Christine. Are you familiar with the term "unconditional love"?

CHRISTINE. Yeah.

MR. SYKES. Would you say you receive this kind of love? At home?

CHRISTINE. Sure.

MR. SYKES. Really? How do you define unconditional love?

CHRISTINE. I get to stay, on the condition that they don't have to love me.

MR. SYKES. Hmm. This is not what I mean.

CHRISTINE. Then what is it?

MR. SYKES. There are many parents that love and support their children, Christine. No matter what mistakes their kids make, or how bad their behavior may be. It doesn't affect how much they love their kids. Their love is unconditional. Understand? *(Pause. Christine stares at him.)*

CHRISTINE. Get real.

MR. SYKES. I'm serious.

CHRISTINE. You *know* people like this?

MR. SYKES. Well. Not personally. But I've read case histories. Let's get back to you. It seems to me you're suffering from a mild depression.

CHRISTINE. No shit, Sherlock.

MR. SYKES. Nothing out of the ordinary for a girl your age. The transition from childhood to adulthood is equivalent to entering a foreign country without knowing the language. It's perfectly normal.

CHRISTINE. So what do you wanna do? Put me on that drug for the hyperactive kids?

MR. SYKES. Ritalin? No. You don't want to be *that* normal. No, I was thinking more along the lines of ... a lobotomy. *(Pause.)*

CHRISTINE. What?

MR. SYKES. It's the quickest way to achieve relief, Christine. If you like, we could start out with a little electroshock, just to calm you down a little. Or maybe we could remove the skullcap and poke around in the old brain matter, prod a few cerebral nerve endings, watch you involuntarily scratch your nose or bark like a dog, that kind of thing. It's good rainy day fun, but a bit of a time waster, don't you think? And I don't have a good hacksaw handy. Not to mention a decent anesthetic. *(He opens a desk drawer and reaches inside.)*

CHRISTINE. Wait a minute. *(Mr. Sykes brings up an electric power drill. He begins to put a very long drill bit into the shaft.)*

MR. SYKES. No, I think it's best just to get to the heart of the matter. One long thrust into the frontal lobe and your problems are solved. Good-bye to depression, good-bye to anger, good-bye to insecurity. And good-bye to Christine, but that's another subject. *(He turns on the drill, which has a terrifying high-speed intensity.)* Just think, you can be happy again. And Mom and Dad will be so proud of you.

CHRISTINE. NO! STOP IT! *(The drill disappears behind the desk, as Mr. Sykes lowers it and quickly brings up an electric pencil sharpener. He is sharpening a pencil.)*

MR. SYKES. What's wrong? *(Christine stares at the pencil sharpener with some confusion.)* My pencil broke. Did I startle you? *(He puts the sharpener down.)* So where were we? Ah yes, Ritalin. I don't think so, Christine. The last thing you need is a stimulant. There are other things we could try, though. *(Christine jumps to her feet and runs off. He calls after her.)* Christine? We didn't set another appointment!

Goal Displacement

Marlys and Christine at the breakfast table. Christine drinks a cola, while Marlys peruses a note from school.

MARLYS. So what exactly *do* you eat for lunch? You never bring anything from home, and evidently you don't care for anything they serve.

CHRISTINE. I eat stuff.

MARLYS. Like what?

CHRISTINE. Fries.

MARLYS. And Cokes. No wonder your behavior is erratic. Your goldfish gets more protein than you do.

CHRISTINE. *(Calling off.)* Dad!

MARLYS. Don't call your father. Tell me what's wrong with the cafeteria food.

CHRISTINE. I don't eat animals.

MARLYS. Surely they serve beans and vegetables. You should have no objections to that.

CHRISTINE. Except it sucks. All their cooks are on prison leave.

MARLYS. You don't know that for sure. *(Josh enters.)*

CHRISTINE. Dad. Tell Mom to stop it.

JOSH. Stop it, Marlys. Christine, I want you to see Grandma after school. I'll drive you to the hospital.

CHRISTINE. I can't.

JOSH. You can take the time. She won't be around that much longer.

CHRISTINE. She doesn't even know I'm there.

JOSH. I know she doesn't seem to respond. But I promise you she's aware when family visits. Besides, duty is not always a pleasant thing. Ask your mother. She's put in her time, haven't you, Marlys?

MARLYS. Fifteen years.

JOSH. I mean at the hospital. How about a little help here?

MARLYS. She can't go, Josh. We have an appointment with the school therapist.

JOSH. Therapist?

MARLYS. She's been showing some unruly behavior at lunch period.

JOSH. So what? That doesn't mean there's something wrong with her.

MARLYS. Don't get bent out of shape. A therapist doesn't mean she's Frances Farmer. He just wants to get at the root of what's really troubling her.

JOSH. Are you troubled, Christine?

CHRISTINE. No.

JOSH. There, see?

MARLYS. So you're just taking her word for it.

JOSH. Why not? I have problems too, but you don't see me running off for professional help at the first aberration. *(Megan enters in a bathrobe, carrying a coffee cup. She sits at the table.)*

MEGAN. Good morning. Sleep well?

MARLYS. Maybe you should, Josh. You and I could profit from a little better communication.

MEGAN. I'd listen to her if I were you.

JOSH. It's none of your business.

MARLYS. You've become one hell of an expert on family matters, Josh. I hope Christine and I are a little more than research for your movie.

MEGAN. Good point.

JOSH. Go away!

MARLYS. Fine with me. *(She exits.)*

CHRISTINE. I hate it when you fight. *(She throws her empty cola can on the floor and follows her mother out.)*

MEGAN. Why exactly am I here, Josh?

JOSH. I was going to ask you the same thing.

MEGAN. Oh, I suspect it's to buff up the old self-image, don't you? To tell you what a tiger you are, it takes a real man to orient me in the right direction, no more gender confusion for this gal, that kind of thing. Sort of pathetic, don't you think? Though this coffee's not bad. Do you have a grinder?

JOSH. I didn't ask you to come here.

MEGAN. No, you didn't. But I'm here just the same. Why do you think that is, Josh?

JOSH. You're mistaken if you think I need you. I don't.

MEGAN. Fine. I'll go away now.
JOSH. Good. *(She doesn't move.)*
MEGAN. More coffee, please.

Discursive Consciousness

Mr. Sykes at his desk, with Marlys and Christine seated facing him.

MR. SYKES. Now, there's nothing about this session which should cause anyone stress or concern. This is a perfectly casual appointment, just to air out whatever feelings may be lying underneath Christine's problems at home and school. Sometimes it's a little easier to discuss your feelings with a dispassionate observer in the same room.
CHRISTINE. This blows. I'm outta here. *(Christine gets up and exits. Marlys and Mr. Sykes watch her go, then turn back to each other.)*
MARLYS. Sorry. Guess we wasted your time.
MR. SYKES. Not yet you haven't. I've still got a half hour scheduled for this. Why don't you stay on and we'll talk.
MARLYS. Is that a good idea? Without her here?
MR. SYKES. It might help get a few things accomplished. Anything you'd like to share with me? Any recent problems at home?
MARLYS. Not really.
MR. SYKES. Anything at all.
MARLYS. Well, my husband's mother is dying.
MR. SYKES. Now see, that alone —
MARLYS. And he's probably thinking about having an affair.
MR. SYKES. That's a significant concern —
MARLYS. And Christine appears to be somewhat anorexic. And worries a lot about sex.
MR. SYKES. Really —
MARLYS. And I'm having trouble staying focused on my consulting business. Probably since I haven't been laid in weeks.
MR. SYKES. Let's take these one at a —

MARLYS. And I keep feeling that I ought to be doing more to keep my family together. But to tell you the truth, I'd rather not hear about their problems. So I'd say things are pretty much coming apart at the seams. Now tell me how all this is typical in modern families.
MR. SYKES. It is, you know.
MARLYS. Because I've been trying so hard, so long, just to keep things normal. For God's sake, don't tell me I've succeeded. This isn't my idea of normal.
MR. SYKES. I don't mean to sound harsh, Mrs. Hauser. But you think your family has problems? What about drug abuse? Alcoholism? Incest? Poverty? At least you've got food on the table.
MARLYS. Which my daughter won't eat.
MR. SYKES. Still. Pardon me if this sounds callous, but your problems are so commonplace as to be considered downright boring. *(Pause.)*
MARLYS. I'm sorry.
MR. SYKES. Don't apologize to me. Forgive yourself. You're punishing yourself for no reason.
MARLYS. I'm getting more like my mother every day.
MR. SYKES. And that scares you?
MARLYS. Oh, that would scare most of humanity.
MR. SYKES. What traits do you think you inherited? What does your mother represent to you?
MARLYS. Other than the systematic crushing of dreams? Let me think.
MR. SYKES. What dreams are those?
MARLYS. Wait a minute. Shouldn't we be talking about Christine?
MR. SYKES. Maybe we are. Sometimes it's a matter of getting back to the source.
MARLYS. Trust me. You don't want to go there.
MR. SYKES. Growing up in your family —
MARLYS. Is not something I would recommend.
MR. SYKES. Tell me about them.
MARLYS. Well, my father was a movie buff. His favorite movie was the same as Howard Hughes' — *Ice Station Zebra.*
MR. SYKES. I'm trying to remember —

MARLYS. Countless scenes of a submarine wending its way through a maze of ice under the North Pole. Which was basically my father's role in our family. Except for, oh yes, this is an important distinction — there's not one woman in that movie.
MR. SYKES. He would have preferred it that way?
MARLYS. I think so. And Rock Hudson at the helm. My dad loved Rock Hudson. He admired men who didn't reveal too much of themselves.
MR. SYKES. And how about your mother?
MARLYS. Once I discovered her cutting all the heads out of the family photo album. And replacing them with heads from magazine ads. She was not what I would call a happy person.
MR. SYKES. Any idea why?
MARLYS. She never said. So I blamed myself.
MR. SYKES. What did you do wrong?
MARLYS. Oh, breathing, existing, that sort of thing. Anything I did could result in profound disappointment. Never punishment — no beatings, that would have been too easy. Instead I got the look.
MR. SYKES. The look.
MARLYS. Imagine Mother Teresa catching you with a vibrator. The look was never accompanied by a word. It just shimmered in its own evil purity. It could cause civil wars. Cancer in laboratory rats.
MR. SYKES. You seem a little worked up, Mrs. Hauser. Perhaps you should calm down.
MARLYS. No thanks. This is great. I don't get to do this at home.
MR. SYKES. How long has it been since you've discussed these issues with anyone?
MARLYS. Let me think. 1976 comes to mind. No, that was the bicentennial.
MR. SYKES. You need to find a release for your frustrations.
MARLYS. You're right. I didn't let you get a word in, did I? Let's talk about you.
MR. SYKES. That's not really the point of this —
MARLYS. I feel like I'm dating again. This is fun. Do you like dancing, holding hands or long walks in the moonlight?

MR. SYKES. Mrs. Hauser. It seems to me that Christine —
MARLYS. Who?
MR. SYKES. Your daughter.
MARLYS. Oh, right.
MR. SYKES. I think she may be reflecting issues within her own family. If a family operates dysfunctionally, it's not unusual for the individual members to develop problems with self-esteem ... trust ... and resentment.
MARLYS. Can you help us?
MR. SYKES. I'm just a school therapist, Mrs. Hauser. Not a psychiatrist. I'm not really qualified to make diagnoses ... for big people.
MARLYS. I had a feeling you didn't have anything in that bag for me. Even if you did help the Scarecrow.
MR. SYKES. Tell you what. Let's make another appointment. And next time you should probably bring your husband.
MARLYS. Do I have to?
MR. SYKES. You don't want him to come?
MARLYS. Well, it sort of ruins that first-date feeling.
MR. SYKES. Think about your daughter, Mrs. Hauser.
MARLYS. Oh, thanks. Now you've really killed the mood.
MR. SYKES. Mrs. Hauser.
MARLYS. You think I'm a bad mother, don't you?
MR. SYKES. I never said anything of the sort. You really like to punish yourself, don't you?
MARLYS. I don't play golf.

Impression Management

A hospital waiting room. Dr. Grey consults a medical chart while she speaks with Josh.

DR. GREY. Well. Her condition remains stable. We're monitoring her organs, keeping her on oxygen and the I.V. feed, checking her pulse and blood pressure, continuing the transfusions, and trying to keep her comfortable. That's pretty much all we can do for now. Until we see a change.

JOSH. What kind of change?

DR. GREY. In either direction.

JOSH. I'm sorry, I don't understand. What exactly is wrong with her?

DR. GREY. We're continuing the tests.

JOSH. You're saying you don't know?

DR. GREY. I'm saying that we are in the process of ruling out possible scenarios.

JOSH. But she's been here for two weeks.

DR. GREY. Which is why I believe we may be getting closer to a diagnosis.

JOSH. But what exactly are you doing to make her *better?*

DR. GREY. As little as possible. *(Pause.)*

JOSH. Say that again?

DR. GREY. Better to be a little cautious, Mr. Hauser. Until we know a little more about exactly what we're trying to cure.

JOSH. You're telling me you're not doing *anything.*

DR. GREY. Medicine is not an exact science. I suggest you read *The Tao of Physics.* You might find it rather calming.

JOSH. Look. I know I'm a layperson. But I'm not a moron. Now I'd like you to tell me, in simple but precise language, what is wrong with my mother. *(Pause.)*

DR. GREY. Her system is being threatened.

JOSH. What system?

DR. GREY. Her system of self-sustenance. The antibodies are down. Her lungs and heart are working overtime. Her immune system appears to be shot. Her body is in the process of giving up. We're just trying to encourage it to hang in there.

JOSH. But how did this start? What made her sick?

DR. GREY. Ah. If we only knew that, we could probably be a little more helpful.

JOSH. But I'm getting bills for all these tests —

DR. GREY. And they're essential to the process. Because they tell us what's not wrong with her.

JOSH. But not what *is.*

DR. GREY. Precisely. *(Pause. Josh rubs his forehead.)* Would you like an aspirin?

JOSH. It just doesn't seem like you're doing enough to help her.

DR. GREY. Mr. Hauser. I would love to hook her up to a full battalion of antibiotics. But for every positive reaction, there are usually adverse side effects. At least we're not making her worse.

JOSH. I'm not so sure about that. She barely responds when I'm here.

DR. GREY. Her body is telling her to heal itself. Family is often a source of physical stress.

JOSH. Are you saying she'd rather not see me?

DR. GREY. Not at all. Of course she wants to see you. She'd just rather you didn't see her.

JOSH. How long will this go on?

DR. GREY. As long as it takes.

JOSH. For what?

DR. GREY. For things to change. Go home and relax, Mr. Hauser. She's not going anywhere.

JOSH. It's just that I wish I could ... do more.

DR. GREY. Don't we all.

Zone of Transition

Josh, Christine and Marlys at the breakfast table. Josh peruses the newspaper while Christine does some last-minute homework. Marlys sips her coffee.

MARLYS. Pass the butter, please. *(No response.)* The butter. *(No response.)* The butter, please. It's next to the jam. *(No response.)* Hello? Anybody there? Can I have the damn butter? *(No response.)* Don't play games, I'm not in the mood. *(Josh glances up at her.)*

JOSH. Christine.

CHRISTINE. What?

JOSH. Your mother wants something.

MARLYS. At last.
CHRISTINE. So?
JOSH. So see what she wants.
MARLYS. The *butter.*
CHRISTINE. How do I do that?
JOSH. Come on, Christine. It's not that difficult. Just be a little patient with her.
MARLYS. If one of you doesn't pass me the goddamn butter — *(Christine turns to Marlys.)*
CHRISTINE. What is it, Mom? What do you want?
MARLYS. The *butter.*
CHRISTINE. You need a spoon?
MARLYS. Don't mess with me, girl. You're stepping over the line.
JOSH. Maybe she wants some sugar for her coffee.
CHRISTINE. You want sugar? Point or something. I'm not a mind reader.
MARLYS. What are you two doing? *(Josh looks up at her and speaks loudly and slowly using hand gestures.)*
JOSH. What IS it dear? What do you WANT?
MARLYS. Don't do this to me.
JOSH. Try the sugar. *(Christine plops the sugar in front of her.)*
CHRISTINE. There. Go to town.
JOSH. Christine —
CHRISTINE. Look, I'm sorry. I just don't know how to talk to her anymore.
JOSH. I know, it's difficult.
CHRISTINE. If only her brain hadn't turned to mush.
JOSH. *Hey* —
CHRISTINE. Well, it's true.
JOSH. It may be true, but it's not a very kind thing to say.
CHRISTINE. Okay, I'm sorry. *(By now Marlys is staring at them wide-eyed.)*
JOSH. There, see? It *was* the sugar. She's calmed down considerably.
CHRISTINE. I wish she could make a little sense.
JOSH. Me too, darling. But those days are over forever.
CHRISTINE. How did it happen, Dad?

JOSH. Oh, it was a gradual process. Nothing we could have prevented. She just sat there, day after day, slowly deteriorating. Her language reduced to nonsensical blather. Like asking for butter. It could have been happening for years.

CHRISTINE. Shouldn't we put her away somewhere?

JOSH. Eventually. Let's allow her a few illusions. For a while, anyway.

CHRISTINE. Oh, no. She's drooling again.

JOSH. You know what to do.

CHRISTINE. Hold still, Mom. I'll get it. *(Christine picks up a napkin and turns to Marlys.)*

MARLYS. Stay away from me! I am not an invalid! *(Josh and Christine stare at her, startled. Christine dabs her own nose with the napkin.)*

JOSH. What the hell's wrong with you?

CHRISTINE. Jesus, Mom. Don't scare us like that. *(She sips her cola.)*

MARLYS. I'm sorry.

JOSH. You okay now? You want anything?

MARLYS. Yes, please. I would like some butter. *(Christine plops the butter in front of her.)*

CHRISTINE. Here.

MARLYS. *Thank* you. *(She spreads some butter on her toast.)*

CHRISTINE. Don't make such a big deal out of it. All you have to do is ask. *(Christine returns to her homework, and Josh returns to his newspaper. Marlys pours some cereal.)*

MARLYS. Please pass the milk. *(No response.)* Milk? Please? *(No one looks up.)*

Time-Space Distanciation

Christine in the hospital waiting room, sitting. Dr. Grey enters and approaches her.

DR. GREY. She's your grandmother, isn't she?

CHRISTINE. Yeah.
DR. GREY. Your father said you might be coming.
CHRISTINE. Not with him. Not 'cause I have to.
DR. GREY. That's understandable. It's a little difficult.
CHRISTINE. Why does she just lie there?
DR. GREY. That's all her body is prepared for at this moment.
CHRISTINE. Will she get better?
DR. GREY. "Better" is a relative term.
CHRISTINE. I mean better than now.
DR. GREY. We're watching her very carefully.
CHRISTINE. For what?
DR. GREY. For an indication. You should probably talk to your father. I already explained it to him in detail.
CHRISTINE. I don't want him to know I was here.
DR. GREY. All right.
CHRISTINE. It's not about him and what he wants. I don't do things just because he wants me to.
DR. GREY. What do *you* want?
CHRISTINE. To talk to Grandma. But I can't even do that. She's a zombie.
DR. GREY. "Zombie" is a relative term.
CHRISTINE. She used to like me. Until I got too old.
DR. GREY. You're hardly what I'd call old.
CHRISTINE. She said she'd rather see me drown before I turned thirteen.
DR. GREY. I'm sure she meant that with affection.
CHRISTINE. I just wish I could talk to her like I used to.
DR. GREY. What would you say to her?
CHRISTINE. I don't know. Just that things are really fucked. And I miss those puzzles she used to bring me. *(Dr. Grey replies with her voice and manner noticeably changed.)*
DR. GREY. That's news to me.
CHRISTINE. What?
DR. GREY. I never got a single thank-you card.
CHRISTINE. Grandma?
DR. GREY. When I was your age we had to write handwritten thank-you notes for everything. We didn't make phone calls to thank our grandmothers for Christmas gifts.

CHRISTINE. God. It's like I can hear her.

DR. GREY. Don't say "God". Unless you're praying for something. And that would be a first for anyone in *this* family.

CHRISTINE. Please don't die, Grandma.

DR. GREY. Oh, quit pouting. What do you want to tell me, anyway? If it's about boys I don't want to hear it. Just watch the talk shows. That's how *I* learn things. Long after I'm dead, that damn television will still be blaring on. Maybe it will receive my spirit.

CHRISTINE. I want to talk about Mom and Dad.

DR. GREY. Oh, Christ. Can't you just smother me with a pillow?

CHRISTINE. Why are they so unhappy?

DR. GREY. Because they think they *shouldn't* be. Why they think *they're* so special, I'll never know. Who told them to expect happiness? Not me, that's for sure.

CHRISTINE. Do they love me?

DR. GREY. In their own way.

CHRISTINE. What does that mean?

DR. GREY. I don't know. It's an empty phrase. Thought it might help.

CHRISTINE. I wish I knew for sure.

DR. GREY. Look, Carol —

CHRISTINE. Christine.

DR. GREY. Heartfelt expressions of love aren't exactly a family trait. I remember a great uncle who tried it back in the thirties. Our family had him committed. Believe me, it's best not to think about it.

CHRISTINE. But I love *you.*

DR. GREY. Of course you do, sweetheart. I'm almost dead. It's permitted.

CHRISTINE. But I mean it. I want you to know. *(Dr. Grey returns to her normal speaking voice and manner.)*

DR. GREY. Too late.

CHRISTINE. No it's not.

DR. GREY. Visiting hours are over.

CHRISTINE. What?

DR. GREY. It's too late for you to be here. Hospital rules.

CHRISTINE. Oh. Okay.

DR. GREY. She'll still be here tomorrow.
CHRISTINE. Is she in pain?
DR. GREY. She's resting comfortably. It's best to come back in the morning.
CHRISTINE. I can't. I have school.
DR. GREY. That's okay. I'm sure she wouldn't want you to interrupt your schedule for her.
CHRISTINE. Yeah. Sure. *(Christine starts to leave. Dr. Grey changes her voice and manner again.)*
DR. GREY. Corrine. *(Christine turns.)*
CHRISTINE. Grandma?
DR. GREY. Don't believe it. The pain is killing me.

Rational Choice Theory

Megan and Josh at the editing machine. They watch the film.

JOSH. See, the question is whether the family, as an institution, is really disintegrating. Or just adapting to changing social conditions. But what *is* a family? Whose definition do you use? And if it really is being threatened, how do you defend it in such a way that appeals to the general population?
MEGAN. So this section deals with historical perspective.
JOSH. Exactly. See, here's the White House Conference on Families. Organized by Jimmy Carter in 1980. They had to change the very title of the conference, from "Family" to "Families," just to keep from ruffling feathers. And although the conference was intended to create a unified family policy, all it caused was more dissension. No one could agree on what the American family was supposed to be.
MEGAN. So there was no family policy. Because the family got lost in the shuffle.
JOSH. Exactly. The fight for the family has mutated into a battle between conflicting visions of public culture. *(Megan rises from the editing machine.)*

MEGAN. This is good, Josh. Do you have enough footage? *(Josh stands up.)*

JOSH. More than enough. From Lyndon Johnson to Phyllis Schlafly.

MEGAN. This puts us over the top.

JOSH. It does?

MEGAN. You've given it context and authority. I don't think we'll have any trouble getting a green light for this project.

JOSH. You're not just saying that?

MEGAN. Just keep practicing the pitch.

JOSH. Okay.

MEGAN. And we've got to sit down and do a detailed budget.

JOSH. No problem.

MEGAN. Then I don't see any reason we couldn't get the funding.

JOSH. I'm trying not to get too excited.

MEGAN. Why not? Let yourself go.

JOSH. You've made me so happy, Megan.

MEGAN. You did all the work.

JOSH. The way I feel right now ... I could kiss you.

MEGAN. So why don't you?

JOSH. Huh? *(Megan kisses him. They pull away.)*

MEGAN. Don't think about your wife. *(She kisses him again. They pull away.)* Don't think about your wife.

JOSH. Please ...

MEGAN. Please what? *(She kisses him again. They pull away.)* Don't think about your wife.

JOSH. Do you mind?

MEGAN. Mind what?

JOSH. Not saying that.

MEGAN. I'm not saying anything. Now how about getting your mind back on the subject. *(She kisses him again. Marlys enters and watches.)*

MARLYS. Don't think about your wife. *(Josh pulls away.)*

JOSH. Look. Can we ... just talk for a minute?

MEGAN. It's your wife, isn't it? *(Josh sees Marlys touching her nose.)*

JOSH. I'm not sure. *(Marlys sits down at the editing machine and fiddles with the equipment.)*

MEGAN. It's not a problem for me.

JOSH. I just need to ... catch my breath.

MEGAN. Sure. Go ahead. Call home if you like. I'm not going anywhere.

JOSH. She doesn't bother you?

MEGAN. Not really. It's not as though she's in the same room. *(Marlys grabs a length of film and brandishes a large scissors.)*

JOSH. Stop that! *(He rushes to the editing machine and takes the scissors from Marlys. He holds them as Marlys exits, chuckling.)*

MEGAN. Look, clearly you're not ready for this.

JOSH. I'm just a little ... confused.

MEGAN. See, that's the difference between us. I insist on focus in my life. I don't permit distractions. If I don't want phone calls, I use a machine. If I don't want to return phone calls, I have my assistant handle it. And if the phone call is from a lover, I end the relationship. I still have my cat.

JOSH. You're a bit terrifying, you know that?

MEGAN. But ... There *is* a "but" coming, isn't there?

JOSH. You know there is. *(Josh kisses her. Marlys enters again with Christine, holding her hand.)*

CHRISTINE. Awesome.

MARLYS. What'd I tell you?

CHRISTINE. Does he kiss you like that?

MARLYS. I don't remember.

CHRISTINE. Are they using their tongues?

MARLYS. Hmm. I'm not sure. Let's take a closer look. *(Josh pulls away.)*

JOSH. Can we take a break?

MEGAN. You make this sound like a job.

JOSH. Of course not. You know I'm enjoying it.

MEGAN. I do?

JOSH. It's just ... I'm not like you, Megan. I don't compartmentalize things.

MEGAN. Fine. You have another life at home. I'll remember that. I'm just asking if you need to carry it around with you all the time. *(Josh looks at his family. They shrug.)* Let me put it this way. I think this is an interesting development. And it might be worth exploring. Now as for your family, that's your concern.

Not mine. They're not here. I don't know them. So from my point of view ... they don't exist. *(Pause. Marlys and Christine look at each other and exit.)* It's just the two of us. *(They kiss again.)*

Bounded Rationality

Josh, Marlys and Christine sit in chairs across from Mr. Sykes, who is seated at his desk.

MR. SYKES. I'd like to try a little game.
JOSH. Let me guess. To help us get in touch with our feelings. Right?
MR. SYKES. Not exactly. I'm less interested in your personal feelings than your perceptions of how the others feel.
CHRISTINE. That's easy. They wish I were dead.
MARLYS. That's not true. *You* wish you were dead.
CHRISTINE. You'd like that, wouldn't you?
MR. SYKES. See, we shouldn't be so quick to dismiss anyone's perceptions. If that's how Christine sees it, she has a right to her feelings.
CHRISTINE. Not according to them.
MR. SYKES. All right, Christine. What do you think it would take?
CHRISTINE. For what?
MR. SYKES. For you to change their perceptions of you.
CHRISTINE. I don't get you.
MR. SYKES. See, this is the game. Let's just pretend — for the next few minutes — that you'll give them exactly what they want. Act the way you think they want you to act. Say the things you think they want you to say.
CHRISTINE. No fucking way.
JOSH. Watch your mouth. What do you want this man to think of us?
MR. SYKES. See. That doesn't matter.
JOSH. It doesn't?

CHRISTINE. *I'm* not gonna do it. I'd rather choke on my own puke.

MR. SYKES. I'm not asking you to do it for real. We're just pretending — to see what it's like. Your parents will do the same thing.

JOSH. With Christine?

MR. SYKES. And your wife too. Try bending over backwards. Your only goal will be to please each other. Forget about your own feelings for a while.

MARLYS. I thought you said this would be different.

MR. SYKES. Give it a try, Mrs. Hauser. *(Marlys faces her husband. Pause.)*

MARLYS. Just give him what he wants.

MR. SYKES. That's the idea.

MARLYS. *(Flatly.)* You're a brilliant artist. I'm in awe of your talents.

JOSH. Oh, come on.

MR. SYKES. Your husband doesn't want exaggeration, Mrs. Hauser. What do you think he'd *really* like from you?

MARLYS. I don't know.

MR. SYKES. I think you do.

MARLYS. All right. Support, I guess. And a certain amount of freedom.

MR. SYKES. Don't tell me. Tell your husband. *(Pause.)*

MARLYS. *(To Josh.)* You shouldn't worry so much about us. Go off and do your work. Don't let us distract you. We don't want to be millstones.

CHRISTINE. What's a millstone?

JOSH. Not you, Christine.

MARLYS. A burden.

JOSH. Is that really how you feel?

MARLYS. Well, it's what you think, isn't it?

CHRISTINE. I'm sorry, Dad. I'll try to stay out of your way.

JOSH. That's not what I want, Christine.

CHRISTINE. It's not?

JOSH. Of course not. You're my daughter. You and your mother are my priorities. But I know I've been neglectful. I can be very selfish.

CHRISTINE. No, I'm the one who's selfish.
MARLYS. Why would you say such a thing, dear?
CHRISTINE. I shouldn't cut holes in all the clothes you buy me.
MARLYS. Why not? Josh and I could learn a few things from your value system. We put way too much emphasis on appearances.
JOSH. That's right. I want you to be an independent thinker. Even if I don't always act like it.
MARLYS. Don't put yourself down, Josh. You're a wonderful father.
JOSH. When my work becomes more important than my own family? That's not right.
MARLYS. Of course it is. You should take pride in your talents, Josh. It's one of the many reasons I love you. If I were a better wife I'd be able to say that to you.
JOSH. You are the best wife any man could hope for.
CHRISTINE. I'm sorry I'm such a bitch. I don't mean to hurt you. I love you both.
JOSH. No man deserves the wealth of happiness that this family gives me every day of my life.
MARLYS. You deserve it, Josh.
CHRISTINE. Can I hug you, Mom?
MARLYS. Come here. *(Christine and Marlys hug.)*
JOSH. Now *this* is what I call a family! *(All three hug tearfully. Long pause as they compose themselves. They disengage and take their seats, focusing contentedly on Mr. Sykes.)*
MR. SYKES. Understand? Good. All right then. Who'd like to start? *(They stare at Mr. Sykes, frowning as he sharpens his pencil.)*

End of Act One.

*Epistemological Break (Intermission)

Is the title as house lights come up.

*As all other titles, entirely optional.

ACT TWO

Deviance Amplification

Marlys at the podium.

MARLYS. Now. As you can see from this chart, there are overwhelmingly negative aspects to the presence of job insecurity in the organization. Accounting for ninety-eight percent of polled responses. For example ... the loss of trust. *(Christine enters and faces Marlys from a distance. She holds another can of cola.)*
CHRISTINE. Why are you always against me? You used to like me more.
MARLYS. There may also develop a loss of pride. The feeling that end results are no longer worth the effort.
CHRISTINE. Go ahead, ignore me. Pretend I'm not even here.
MARLYS. There is also an increase in self-protective behavior.
CHRISTINE. You're a real bitch, you know that?
MARLYS. Back to the chart. Twenty-seven percent indicate a negative effect on quality or productivity.
CHRISTINE. This sucks. I hate being in this family. *(Christine throws her can on the floor.)*
MARLYS. One's immediate response may be to hide mistakes by using temporary solutions. *(She digs a credit card out of her purse and holds it out to Christine.)*
CHRISTINE. Cool. *(Christine dashes up to her and kisses her on the cheek with delight.)* Thanks, Mom. I love you. *(Christine runs off. Marlys beams as she turns back to the audience.)*

MARLYS. Some employees can become very adept at these techniques. Where are we on the chart? Ah, yes. Negative feelings about oneself. A nineteen percent response. *(Mr. Sykes enters and addresses Marlys.)*

MR. SYKES. You really like to punish yourself, don't you?

MARLYS. Under these conditions, it's not uncommon to experience a significant loss of self-esteem.

MR. SYKES. Why do you set yourself up as the perfect example? You must realize that you're doomed from the start.

MARLYS. These feelings will no doubt affect your performance.

MR. SYKES. Go ahead. Let it all out.

MARLYS. Twelve percent suggested other negative emotions.

MR. SYKES. Nothing to be ashamed of.

MARLYS. The internalization of anger. Frustration. Depression.

MR. SYKES. Go on. You know there's more.

MARLYS. Until you just want to explode.

MR. SYKES. Excellent.

MARLYS. *(To Mr. Sykes.)* Shut the hell up, will you? *(Mr. Sykes gives her a thumbs up, and leaves the stage. Pause. Marlys turns back to the audience, mortified.)* To ... demonstrate the point. Finally, two percent of the respondents felt that job insecurity actually served a positive function. Though naturally, their point of view was somewhat self-oriented. *(Josh enters with a dozen roses and hands them to Marlys.)*

JOSH. Hi honey. Just letting you know I've decided to have an affair. So I bought you these roses to compensate. Let me know if you need any postcards from the motel. *(He looks at his watch.)* Gotta run. Love you. *(Josh exits. Pause. Marlys turns to the audience, holding the flowers.)*

MARLYS. May I have the next chart. Please.

Cultural Relativism

Marlys and Josh, at the breakfast table.

JOSH. I think you should go back to your singing career. *(Pause.)*
MARLYS. As opposed to what?
JOSH. It gave you such pleasure. And you were so good at it.
MARLYS. It's not something you can just pick up again, Josh. Not after all these years. You have to keep honing your skills. I'd be starting over.
JOSH. I just wish you had something like that now. To give you a little fulfillment.
MARLYS. I chose a family, Josh. It does the job.
JOSH. Does it really? Or do we just get in the way?
MARLYS. Where did all this come from?
JOSH. I've just been thinking about your needs. You must have needs that Christine and I can't always fill.
MARLYS. Nothing out of the ordinary.
JOSH. I just don't want to keep you from pursuing ... outside interests.
MARLYS. Are you trying to tell me something? Maybe *you're* the one who isn't satisfied.
JOSH. Of course not. I just hope you'll tell me if ... you're not happy.
MARLYS. Every time?
JOSH. You know what I mean. Don't hide the truth from me.
MARLYS. All right. I'm having an affair. *(Pause.)*
JOSH. What?
MARLYS. You *are* in a funk this morning, aren't you. Lighten up, Josh. Don't carry the world on your shoulders.
JOSH. Right.
MARLYS. Have you got an extra twenty? I'll pick up the dry cleaning on the way to work.
JOSH. On the dresser. In my wallet.
MARLYS. Thanks. *(She exits as Christine enters.)*
CHRISTINE. I hate my hair.
JOSH. Why? It looks nice.

CHRISTINE. It *exists.* I want to shave it off.
JOSH. You know, all of these trends you're so obsessed with, they're all going to disappear in another year or two. Kids will be pulling the piercings out of their navels and noses, and using lasers to burn off tattoos. And the skinhead look will be long gone.
CHRISTINE. So that's when I'll grow it back.
JOSH. Is it really that important to you? To be able to fit in to some designated group, just by looking like everyone else?
CHRISTINE. Duh. What have I been *saying.*
JOSH. But you're describing a herd mentality. Wouldn't you rather be perceived as an individual?
CHRISTINE. If everyone else is.
JOSH. I'm talking about *you,* Christine. I want you to be yourself.
CHRISTINE. Well why don't you try being me for a while? See how much fun it is. *(Marlys enters, carrying the wallet. She stares at Josh impassively.)*
JOSH. What is it? What? *(She removes a small colored item from the wallet and tosses it on the table.)*
MARLYS. Care to explain?
CHRISTINE. It's a rubber.
JOSH. That's right, Christine. A condom. Which I brought home to show you. I think you've reached the age when we need to have a frank discussion about personal responsibility.
MARLYS. Brought home from *where?*
JOSH. I bought it.
MARLYS. Out of the pack?
CHRISTINE. They sell single cigarettes at the Mini-Mart.
JOSH. You can't be too careful nowadays. Or too prepared. I'll demonstrate. Hand me that banana.
CHRISTINE. I know how they work, Dad.
JOSH. Good. That wasn't too difficult. Here you go. *(He hands Christine the condom.)*
MARLYS. Give it back to him, Christine. You're not ready for it.
CHRISTINE. I don't want it anyway. I'm never gonna have sex as long as I live. *(She tosses it on the table.)*
JOSH. I have no problem with that.

MARLYS. You have some strange misconceptions, dear. Sex is a natural function of life. An expression of mature love. When two people have made an exclusive, long-term commitment to each other. It's not for temporary flings and infatuations.
CHRISTINE. Don't tell me, the angels come down and watch.
MARLYS. Oh, there are others watching, all right.
JOSH. She says she's not interested. I see no reason to pursue this.
CHRISTINE. Do you and Dad use these things?
MARLYS. Of course not. They're only used if one's partner is a total stranger. Someone whose sexual history is questionable or unknown. That's why your father would have no conceivable reason for carrying one of these on his person. Other than the reason he provided.
JOSH. I'm not advocating its use, Christine. I just think it's better to be safe than sorry. So when you find yourself ... needing protection ...
MARLYS. Go on, Josh. This is not a subject to be hesitant about.
JOSH. You'll know what to do. I'll just leave this ... here. Next to the fruit bowl. So when you're ready ... you can practice.
CHRISTINE. I'm not going to need it. I've decided I'm a lesbian.
MARLYS. You are?
CHRISTINE. Sure. They're the most popular. *(She exits.)*

Resistance Through Ritual

Christine is seated opposite Mr. Sykes, in his office. She sips a cola.

CHRISTINE. So I'm in this room full of people I hate.
MR. SYKES. I take it this is a big room.
CHRISTINE. Like a train station. There's Mr. Mosley, who asked me if I had attention deficit disorder — right in front of the whole class. And Mrs. Shank, who said I should make more

of an effort to look feminine. And Paula Rieger, who taped pictures of raw meat to my locker. And Bobby Lacone, who said I have no tits. So I start with Bobby. See, I've got this huge bucket full of bugs —

MR. SYKES. Bugs?

CHRISTINE. Yeah, like worms and slugs and black widow spiders and poisonous centipedes, and I'm trying to pour it all down his throat. I mean, he's all tied up and everything, so it shouldn't be too hard, but he keeps his mouth closed tight. Then Jesus floats down from heaven, right through the ceiling, and all these rainbows appear and cool trumpet music plays, and he looks at me and says, in this really deep and mysterious voice, "You seem troubled, my child." And Jesus grabs Bobby's head and forces his mouth open so I can pour, and before you know it he's got bugs crawling out his nose and ears, and stinging his eyeballs, and his head blows up to the size of a watermelon, and ...

MR. SYKES. How often do you have this dream?

CHRISTINE. Dream? I don't *have* dreams.

MR. SYKES. So it's a story ...

CHRISTINE. For English Lit.

MR. SYKES. This is homework?

CHRISTINE. Yeah, you like it?

MR. SYKES. So what we have here is a long sequence of grisly tortures.

CHRISTINE. That's right.

MR. SYKES. All with the homicidal assistance of Jesus Christ.

CHRISTINE. Sure, he's got the time.

MR. SYKES. Until everyone's dead, I assume.

CHRISTINE. How'd you know?

MR. SYKES. It's the genre.

CHRISTINE. What's that mean?

MR. SYKES. Nothing. A little joke.

CHRISTINE. You making fun of me?

MR. SYKES. No. Not at all.

CHRISTINE. Yes you are. You think it's bad, don't you?

MR. SYKES. Absolutely not. It's completely normal for a girl your age to have revenge fantasies.

CHRISTINE. It's not a fantasy. It's a story. For class.

MR. SYKES. Of course.

CHRISTINE. You're the one who has fantasies. About my mother.

MR. SYKES. How did ... where did this come from?

CHRISTINE. She talks about you all the time, you know.

MR. SYKES. That's not true and you know it.

CHRISTINE. Sure it is. She doesn't get any at home. So she talks about you.

MR. SYKES. Christine —

CHRISTINE. How much she wants you. She's hot for you.

MR. SYKES. This is not funny.

CHRISTINE. She asked me if you had a girlfriend. *(Long pause.)*

MR. SYKES. Did she really? *(Long pause.)*

CHRISTINE. No. *(She smiles.)*

MR. SYKES. So it's a lie.

CHRISTINE. I call it fantasy.

MR. SYKES. Why do you resort to cruelty? Do you really enjoy hurting people?

CHRISTINE. I don't know.

MR. SYKES. Is it because you expect people to hurt *you?*

CHRISTINE. Are we almost done?

MR. SYKES. One more thing. *(He reaches into his desk and pulls out a series of inkblots. He holds one up for her to see.)* What do you see here?

CHRISTINE. An inkblot.

MR. SYKES. Yes, I've heard that one before. Now just tell me the first thing that pops into your mind. What does the picture suggest to you? *(Josh enters and stands behind Mr. Sykes.)*

JOSH. You're my special girl, Christine. You could never, ever disappoint me. No matter how hard you try. That's why I expect such great things from you. Because you're capable of the best. Do you know how much I love you? You couldn't possibly know. As long as you live, you'll never know how much. I'll never go away.

MR. SYKES. That's it, Christine. Good concentration. Now — tell me what you're thinking about. *(Josh exits as Marlys enters the room.)*

MARLYS. How's it going?

CHRISTINE. I told you not to come here. Do you want to scar me for life?

MARLYS. I'm just giving you a ride home.

CHRISTINE. Don't bother. I'm walking. *(She throws her empty Coke can on the floor of Mr. Sykes' office and storms out. Marlys picks up the can apologetically.)*

MARLYS. It's empty. *(Mr. Sykes takes the can from her and puts it on his desk.)*

MR. SYKES. It's customary to knock, Mrs. Hauser.

MARLYS. See, I'd forgotten that. Our house, you know.

MR. SYKES. It's important to keep a professional atmosphere. For example, I always wear a tie. Although there are times I'd like to take it off and use it to strangle the child sitting across from me ... not your daughter of course.

MARLYS. How's she doing?

MR. SYKES. Well ...

MARLYS. Or are you allowed to tell me?

MR. SYKES. Like I told you before. I'm just a therapist. No code of honor here. *(Pause.)* That's a joke.

MARLYS. Oh.

MR. SYKES. Obviously a bad one. I'm sorry.

MARLYS. It's not your fault. I don't recognize jokes anymore. Or compliments. Or salutations. People have conversations with me and I don't know who they're talking to. I keep thinking there's someone else in the room. Have you ever heard of that?

MR. SYKES. Well, I'd have to explore the symptoms, of course. But it sounds like a typical dissociative experience.

MARLYS. Does it mean I'm going crazy?

MR. SYKES. Not at all. The fact that you know you're being irrational suggests that you are rational.

MARLYS. Then if I know I'm being rational I'm being irrational?

MR. SYKES. No. You're being irrational if you don't know you're being irrational. *(Pause.)* I can look it up.

MARLYS. I feel like I'm fading from view. Becoming transparent. Or mutating into something else entirely.

MR. SYKES. I can see you perfectly well.

MARLYS. I'm sure you see *something*. Not necessarily me.

MR. SYKES. Now, Mrs. Hauser —

MARLYS. I'm serious. I've lost confidence that I'm really here.

MR. SYKES. All right. Do you have a photo of yourself? Just something to look at to get beyond this temporary anxiety attack. *(She digs her wallet out of her purse. She pulls out a small photo and examines it.)*

MARLYS. Nope. Don't know her.

MR. SYKES. Give it here. *(He takes it and looks at it.)* Where are you? Standing behind this woman next to your husband?

MARLYS. I *am* the woman next to my husband. *(Mr. Sykes squints at it.)*

MR. SYKES. Maybe it's the lighting ...

MARLYS. Do you want to see my driver's license? *(Mr. Sykes hands the picture back.)*

MR. SYKES. No need. I can give you my complete assurance that you are you.

MARLYS. And who is that?

MR. SYKES. An accomplished, desirable woman who is just feeling a bit insecure right now.

MARLYS. Really? You think I'm desirable?

MR. SYKES. And accomplished. That's my opinion.

MARLYS. You're sweet.

MR. SYKES. Well ... I don't know about that ...

MARLYS. If you're not careful, I'm going to develop a crush on you.

MR. SYKES. Ah. Well. Hmm.

MARLYS. By the way, did Christine tell you ... oh, shit, this is so embarrassing.

MR. SYKES. Go on. Please.

MARLYS. I asked her ... about you.

MR. SYKES. You did? You really did?

MARLYS. She didn't mention it?

MR. SYKES. Well, yes, as a matter of fact. But I didn't know whether to believe her.

MARLYS. Oh no. I've insulted you.

MR. SYKES. Not at all. It was a very welcome ... inquiry.

MARLYS. Oh, good. Because talking about these things ... it's not easy for me.

MR. SYKES. Me either.

MARLYS. So then ... you're free?

MR. SYKES. Yes. Oh yes. Absolutely free. Completely free.

MARLYS. I'm so glad.

MR. SYKES. Me too.

MARLYS. Because I can't afford these sessions. *(Pause.)*

MR. SYKES. How's that?

MARLYS. We're stretching our budget as it is. So if you were to charge for Christine's therapy ... well, it would be a hardship. You understand.

MR. SYKES. Not to worry. The tuition covers it.

MARLYS. Good. I know it's silly, but I get so embarrassed over things like this. You can't imagine.

MR. SYKES. I think I can.

Environmental Depletion

A lakeside. Marlys and Christine are spreading a picnic.

CHRISTINE. Why do we have to do this?

MARLYS. It makes your father happy. Is there something you'd rather do?

CHRISTINE. Slit my wrists.

MARLYS. That's not funny.

CHRISTINE. No shit.

MARLYS. Please, Christine. Can you find it in yourself to be friendly for one afternoon?

CHRISTINE. Buy a dog.

MARLYS. And don't eat all those cookies before lunch.

CHRISTINE. I'm not going to eat those grotesque steaks.

MARLYS. I brought you some pasta salad.

CHRISTINE. Ow! The mosquitoes are eating me alive. Dad *would* have to pick a lake. *(Marlys hands Christine a tube of insect repellent.)*

MARLYS. Here. Use it sparingly. *(Christine spreads huge gobs of insect cream all over her face and arms.) Sparingly.* What's the matter with you?

CHRISTINE. Don't blame me for this stupid picnic. *(Josh enters, carrying a portable grill.)*

JOSH. What the hell is that smell?

MARLYS. We have a toxic daughter on our hands.

CHRISTINE. The bugs are *killing* me.

JOSH. You only need a dab of that stuff.

MARLYS. I told her.

CHRISTINE. Why did we have to come here, Dad? People are looking at us like we're geeks.

JOSH. That's because picnics are a lost art. Someday anthropologists will try to reconstruct picnic grounds as though they were Egyptian burial sites. Petrified deviled eggs will become unexplainable icons from an ancient society.

CHRISTINE. You are so weird.

JOSH. I just think it's about time this family did something as a unit, something that doesn't involve therapists. Let's just experience a little togetherness. And sit further away.

MARLYS. Josh.

JOSH. She'll poison the food.

CHRISTINE. Fine with me. Maybe no one will know I'm with you. *(Christine grabs some cookies and sits further away.)*

MARLYS. Someone's waving at you, Josh.

JOSH. Where?

MARLYS. She's coming over. *(Megan enters, holding an extremely long leash, which extends offstage.)*

MEGAN. Hi Josh.

JOSH. Hi. What are you doing here?

MEGAN. Just taking Evita for a walk. She likes to sit in the reeds and look at the red-winged blackbirds. *(To Marlys.)* I'm Megan Lone. Josh's producer.

MARLYS. Oh, for the documentary?

MEGAN. That's right. It's a wonderful piece. Is this your daughter?

MARLYS. Christine, say hello. She gives your father money.

CHRISTINE. Hello.

JOSH. So. What *brings* you here?

MEGAN. I wanted to show Marlys some snapshots of us having sex.

JOSH. What? *(Megan hands the photos to Marlys.)*

MARLYS. Say, these are good. Did you use a professional?

MEGAN. The neighbor's kid. Developed them himself. He's applying to art school, you know.

MARLYS. He should have no problem getting accepted.

CHRISTINE. So how often do you fuck my dad?

JOSH. Christine!

MEGAN. Fairly regularly. Now *there's* something to show your friends. *(She hands Christine a couple photos.)*

CHRISTINE. Thanks.

JOSH. Jesus Christ.

MARLYS. Calm down, Josh. He gets squeamish about certain subjects.

MEGAN. You're telling me. Do you use a diaphragm?

MARLYS. Of course.

MEGAN. Does he make you do it in the bathroom?

MARLYS. Every time. Strange, don't you think?

MEGAN. I did it in front of him once.

MARLYS. Let me guess. He got soft.

MEGAN. You better believe it. *(They laugh knowingly.)*

CHRISTINE. Dad can't get it up?

MARLYS. On occasion. But let's stop teasing the poor man.

JOSH. I'm ... what are you ... I'm not sure ...

MARLYS. You're being incoherent, dear. Megan, would you like some cheese?

MEGAN. That would be lovely.

MARLYS. I'll cut you some. Josh, are you all right? You look green.

JOSH. It's the ... bug stuff.

MARLYS. Our daughter overdid it with the pest repellent.

MEGAN. Can't get rid of me that easy. Right, Josh?

MARLYS. Here, grab some havarti. *(Megan reaches for the cheese as Marlys cuts another hunk.)* Oops, that was careless of me. I seem to have cut off three of your fingers.

MEGAN. Happens all the time. I'm always putting my fingers where they don't belong.
MARLYS. Would you like a napkin? It would soak up the blood.
MEGAN. That would be nice.
CHRISTINE. Are you going to have a baby?
MEGAN. I don't think so, Christine. But you never know. Your father tells me you weren't exactly part of the plan yourself.
CHRISTINE. Really? *(She turns to Josh.)* I always thought so.
MEGAN. I suggested a picnic, you know. For the two of us. But he claimed not to have enough time.
MARLYS. Christine and I tend to eat into his schedule.
MEGAN. True. It would be more convenient if he didn't have to keep going home to you.
MARLYS. Maybe we can work something out. What would be satisfactory, Josh?
JOSH. I'm not ... feeling well. *(They both feel his forehead simultaneously.)*
MEGAN. He does feel warm.
MARLYS. Funny. Feels cold to me.
CHRISTINE. Hey, lady. Your cat's barfing.
MEGAN. Oh, she's fine. She's just been eating some grass. Animals purge themselves in order to purify their systems. I better take her home now. May I have my fingers back?
MARLYS. May I keep one? I'm short on spoons for the onion dip.
MEGAN. Certainly. It's been a pleasure to meet you at last. I never realized you had such a lovely family, Josh. Be sure to let me know when you've finally ditched them.
MARLYS. Take care.
CHRISTINE. Bye.
MEGAN. Take care. *(Megan moves off.)*
MARLYS. *(To Josh.)* Well, you were the quiet one.
JOSH. Nothing ... to say.
MARLYS. I thought she was very nice. Didn't you, Christine?
CHRISTINE. She's okay. Not as boring as most of Dad's friends.
MARLYS. There you are, Josh. Praise indeed from your daughter.

JOSH. Let's go home.
CHRISTINE. Yay. Finally.
MARLYS. We haven't even had lunch. Are you still feeling sick?
CHRISTINE. Maybe he should eat some grass.
JOSH. Home. Please ... just take me home.

Frustration-Aggression Hypothesis

Josh and Megan in the editing room.

JOSH. Walking a cat? Who the hell walks *cats*?
MEGAN. I do.
JOSH. But why the lake? There must be a hundred other places to go.
MEGAN. No there aren't. It's the *lake.* Everybody goes to the lake. It's taken for granted. If you go anywhere, you go to the lake. Evita likes the lake. Evidently, even *you* like the lake. *(Pause.)* All right; I got curious. I wanted to step into your other life for a moment. I didn't mean to intrude.
JOSH. Then why did you?
MEGAN. I don't know. You shouldn't have told me your plans for the weekend.
JOSH. Don't worry. I won't from now on.
MEGAN. It's all over anyway.
JOSH. What's over?
MEGAN. Stop it, Josh. *We're* over. You *know* we're over.
JOSH. I don't know that.
MEGAN. I met your family. Now they're as real to me as they are to you. Probably more so. I can't do this anymore. I won't do it.
JOSH. You said you didn't care.
MEGAN. They were imaginary figures. But now they're real. Don't you see how that makes a difference?
JOSH. They belong to me. Not you.

MEGAN. Look, I'll admit it. I probably got off on the fantasy. The secret life of Josh Hauser. I guess I enjoyed being that secret. But not now. The fantasy's over.

JOSH. You can't decide that.

MEGAN. I just did.

JOSH. I'm the one who's supposed to decide that.

MEGAN. Fine. Go ahead. If it makes you feel better. Pretend to be the noble husband and father.

JOSH. It's not a pretense.

MEGAN. Final seconds! Last chance to score. The buzzer sounds, but the ball's in motion, and ... Yes! It's good! A last-minute victory for Josh Hauser! He breaks up with his mistress! What a hero! Break out the Gatorade! *(Pause.)* Feel better now?

JOSH. You don't care about my family. You're just using this as an excuse.

MEGAN. I don't need an excuse, Josh. This was a mistake from the start. Know why? You never really wanted me. You wanted your family. Oh, you do a good show with this movie of yours, claiming to expose the hypocrisy of the conventional American family. Finding all this old footage and making fun of it. But now I know why you're so obsessed with traditional myths. You want them *back.* Having picnics on the lake with your devoted wife and well-adjusted daughter.

JOSH. Don't talk to me about family. You don't know the first thing about it. Except for your postmodern, gender-bending, non-nuclear "alternatives." Give me a break.

MEGAN. Oh, I forgot, you're the expert on family values. That's why you spent three afternoons a week at *my* house. *(Pause. Josh goes to the editing machine and starts to wind the reel.)*

JOSH. Send me the rest when it comes back from the lab.

MEGAN. Don't do this, Josh. We can still work together.

JOSH. Not in this lifetime.

MEGAN. Okay, I flew off. I'm sorry. I have feelings too, you know.

JOSH. Since when? *(He pulls the reels off the editing machine and storms out of the office. Megan stands there, looking after him. She turns off the machine, and begins to clean up coffee cups and assorted trash. Marlys enters.)*

MARLYS. Hello again.

MEGAN. Mrs. Hauser?

MARLYS. Is my husband around? I thought we could grab some lunch. But I'm probably too early.

MEGAN. You just missed him.

MARLYS. Maybe I could wait?

MEGAN. I'm not ... sure when he'll be ... back.

MARLYS. Oh, I know he's busy. He's very preoccupied. I know it has to do with work.

MEGAN. Yes.

MARLYS. Although for I while I thought ... I guess I should ... Can I tell you a secret? More of a confession, really.

MEGAN. If you ... like.

MARLYS. I thought Josh might be having an affair. *(Pause.)*

MEGAN. I'm not sure this is something I should —

MARLYS. Oh, but this has to do with you. See, I had been thinking you were the one. *(Pause.)*

MEGAN. I see. Well ...

MARLYS. But it's okay now. Josh explained it to me.

MEGAN. He did.

MARLYS. You know, about you.

MEGAN. I'm not sure I —

MARLYS. That it couldn't possibly be you. Because of how you are.

MEGAN. How ... am I?

MARLYS. You know ... you're gay, right? *(Pause.)*

MEGAN. *(Bitterly.)* Right.

MARLYS. So I'm sorry if I seemed a little strange at the lake.

MEGAN. Not at all. You were perfectly nice.

MARLYS. That's a relief. I won't even tell you what kind of strange thoughts were passing through my mind.

MEGAN. Perfectly understandable.

MARLYS. Until Josh set me straight. Well ... tell him I dropped by. *(She turns to leave.)*

MEGAN. Mrs. Hauser?

MARLYS. Please. Call me Marlys.

MEGAN. Marlys ... This is a little too easy.

MARLYS. Easy?

MEGAN. It's not fair to you. Or to me. *(Pause.)*
MARLYS. Oh, shit.
MEGAN. There have been women in my past. And men as well.
MARLYS. Including my husband. *(She slowly sits.)*
MEGAN. It never really got off the ground. His heart was always with you.
MARLYS. It's not his heart I'm thinking about.
MEGAN. I won't be seeing him anymore. And it looks like our project fell apart.
MARLYS. I think I should be allowed not to care about that for the moment.
MEGAN. Of course.
MARLYS. Nothing seems to matter anymore.
MEGAN. How about if I buy you lunch?
MARLYS. It doesn't matter.
MEGAN. Come on. I think it would help. *(They stand to go. Marlys suddenly stops.)*
MARLYS. Wait a minute. I'm sure you're a perfectly nice person, but I don't feel like being your friend. Not today, anyway.
MEGAN. All right.
MARLYS. You just can't do things like that. Step into other people's lives — people you don't even *know* — and fuck around with their happiness.
MEGAN. I know. I'm sorry. *(Pause.)*
MARLYS. Okay. Let's have lunch.

Episodic Characterization

Marlys at the breakfast table, reading the newspaper and eating an English muffin. Christine enters, drinking a cola.

CHRISTINE. Morning.
MARLYS. Have an English muffin.
CHRISTINE. I'm not hungry.
MARLYS. Sleep well?

CHRISTINE. Okay, I guess. How long does Dad have to sleep on the couch?

MARLYS. I don't know.

CHRISTINE. What did he do this time? It must have been a major boner.

MARLYS. None of your business.

CHRISTINE. Don't tell me he's screwing around on you.

MARLYS. Christine —

CHRISTINE. Just don't stay together on my account. That would truly suck.

MARLYS. Nobody's getting divorced.

CHRISTINE. Only ninety-five percent of the human race. But go ahead, be miserable for no reason.

MARLYS. We'll discuss this when you get home from school.

CHRISTINE. I'll be home late. I'm joining a club.

MARLYS. Well, this is wonderful news, Christine. I've been hoping you'd take up an extra-curricular activity. What kind of club is it?

CHRISTINE. A new one. We meet after school.

MARLYS. Excellent. Just call if it gets too late. Sure you won't eat a muffin? *(Pause. Christine picks up a muffin and smells it.)*

CHRISTINE. I'll take it with me.

MARLYS. Good for you, dear. *(Christine exits. Marlys returns to her newspaper. Megan enters in a bathrobe and sits at the table.)*

MEGAN. Good morning.

MARLYS. Have an English muffin.

MEGAN. Don't mind if I do.

MARLYS. Sleep well?

MEGAN. I think you know the answer to that.

MARLYS. Are we sleeping together now?

MEGAN. No. Not yet.

MARLYS. I didn't think so.

MEGAN. But you're giving it a lot of thought.

MARLYS. I might just be mad at Josh.

MEGAN. That's true.

MARLYS. Or I may just need a change.

MEGAN. Also possible.

MARLYS. You realize I don't have the guts to act on this.

MEGAN. That's why I'm here.
MARLYS. I have to think of my daughter.
MEGAN. Of course you do.
MARLYS. Still, it doesn't seem fair that everyone else gets to have an adventure.
MEGAN. While you're stuck with your sense of duty.
MARLYS. You're very understanding.
MEGAN. As long as you want me to be. *You* realize that in real life, I don't give two shits about your problems.
MARLYS. I know. You have your cat.
MEGAN. As long as we understand each other. Good muffin.
MARLYS. Thank you. *(Megan and Marlys return to their newspapers. Mr. Sykes enters in a bathrobe and sits at the table.)*
MR. SYKES. Good morning.
MARLYS. Have an English muffin.
MR. SYKES. No thank you.
MARLYS. Sleep well?
MR. SYKES. I think you know the answer to that. *(Marlys and Megan exchange a knowing smile.)* Mrs. Hauser, I'm here to inform you that this household is an unfit environment to bring up a child.
MARLYS. I see. So you're planning to take Christine away from me?
MR. SYKES. Not really. I'm just contributing to your sense of failure.
MARLYS. I appreciate it.
MR. SYKES. Personally, I wish you wouldn't think of me in such an authoritarian way. To tell you the truth, I find you damned attractive.
MARLYS. But in a safe way.
MR. SYKES. Absolutely. If that's how you want it.
MARLYS. I think that's best.
MR. SYKES. Anything new to report?
MARLYS. Christine took a muffin with her.
MR. SYKES. Really? That *is* progress. I'll try one now. *(He bites into one.)*
MARLYS. How is it?
MR. SYKES. Undercooked. She'll probably hate it. *(Mr. Sykes*

picks up a newspaper, along with Marlys and Megan. Josh enters.)

JOSH. Good morning. *(Marlys does not look up from her paper.)* Are those English muffins? *(No response. He grabs one.)* Sleep well? *(He bites into the muffin.)* Could use a little more time in the toaster. *(Marlys puts down the paper and stands up.)* It's good though. See? I'm eating it. *(Marlys begins to leave.)* Marlys? *(She stops and turns, staring at him impassively.)* How long can this go on? I'm in limbo here. I'm home but not home. Married but not married. You don't even tell me what's going on around here.

MARLYS. Congratulations. Now you know how it feels to be Marlys Hauser.

JOSH. All I'm saying is —

MARLYS. Hold on a second. *(Megan and Mr. Sykes glance at each other. They stand up and exit, giving Marlys gestures of encouragement on the way out. Marlys turns back to Josh.)* I don't have any answers for you, Josh.

JOSH. I know I deserve your anger.

MARLYS. And so much more.

JOSH. Can we have a normal conversation? Is that too much to ask?

MARLYS. It always has been.

JOSH. It's just that I'm ... floundering here. Hanging around the house, without any sense of purpose. I need some sort of project.

MARLYS. There's always the Peace Corps.

JOSH. Something a little closer to home.

MARLYS. What about your documentary?

JOSH. I can't seem to get a handle on it. I'm giving up on the family idea.

MARLYS. No surprise there.

JOSH. You know what I mean. Don't twist my words.

MARLYS. I'm not the one twisting here.

JOSH. I just want to find some way to be useful. To you and Christine.

MARLYS. Well, we don't need your charity, Josh. Take it elsewhere. Work in a soup kitchen. Go visit the sick. *(She exits. Pause. Dr Grey enters, in her white coat.)*

DR. GREY. Good morning.

Stratificational Models of Social Action and Consciousness

Dr. Grey and Josh, in the hospital.

DR. GREY. I just want you to know that we did everything in our power to make her last moments comfortable.
JOSH. As opposed to actually *helping* her.
DR. GREY. Mr. Hauser. You have odd notions about modern medicine. Life spans can be artificially extended by a number of years, it's true. But is that always a good thing?
JOSH. You wouldn't ask that if it were *your* mother.
DR. GREY. Yes. I would. *(Pause.)*
JOSH. Know what I think? You're a monster in a doctor's costume, that's what I think. With your medical doublespeak and your condescending attitude. As though I'm too stupid to understand what's happening to my own *family*. I know more than you think I know. I can recognize pain, even if they tell you they're feeling fine. I know when they're coherent and when they're spouting nonsense. I know what makes them feel better. Because they'll *tell* me. Not you. Not some stranger probing at them with tubes and needles. They are my *loved* ones. I am the one for whom they will get *better.*
DR. GREY. Then it's too bad you left her in our hands, isn't it? *(Pause.)*
JOSH. How dare you? *(Pause.)* How fucking dare you say that to me? You have no right. You don't know the first thing about me.
DR. GREY. Nor do I care to, so if you'll excuse me —
JOSH. No right at all! *(He calls after her as she leaves. Marlys enters simultaneously.)*
MARLYS. It's okay, Josh. She's doing okay. *(Josh turns and stares at her.)*
JOSH. What are you talking about? She's dead.
MARLYS. Who told you such a thing? No wonder you're so upset.
JOSH. She's still alive?

MARLYS. She's fine. Just a little beat-up, that's all.

JOSH. But I *saw* her. She had no pulse. *(Pause.)*

MARLYS. You're talking about your mother.

JOSH. I saw her.

MARLYS. Oh, Josh. I'm so sorry. *(She hugs him. He pulls away from her, confused.)*

JOSH. Wait a minute. Who are *you* talking about?

MARLYS. I thought the school called you.

JOSH. School? *(Mr. Sykes pushes Christine on in a wheelchair. She appears to have been in a fight, heavily bruised and hair mussed, with a few scratches.)*

MR. SYKES. She's all set to go now.

JOSH. Christine? What's wrong?

CHRISTINE. Nothing. I don't even need this thing.

MARLYS. It's just hospital policy, dear.

MR. SYKES. Ah, Mr. Hauser. Glad you could come. We had a devil of a time reaching you.

JOSH. I've been here all day. What's going on?

MR. SYKES. Well, apparently Christine took part in some sort of gang initiation.

MARLYS. They checked for internal bleeding. She's fine.

MR. SYKES. Still, you should probably keep her home for a few days.

JOSH. Get away from her. *(Josh pushes Mr. Sykes away and kneels in front of Christine.)* A gang? Sweetheart. Why would you want to join a gang? *(Pause. Christine doesn't look at him.)*

CHRISTINE. I was lonely. *(Long pause.)*

JOSH. Lonely? Lonely? Honey, we are your *family*. How could you possibly be lonely with us in your life?

CHRISTINE. Look, I'm sorry, okay? It was a dumb thing to do.

JOSH. What did they do to you?

CHRISTINE. They just hit me with socks filled with dirt. No big deal.

JOSH. No big deal? Why would you *want* others to abuse you? Is that how much you think of yourself?

MR. SYKES. Mr. Hauser. She's had a rough day. Perhaps there's another time for this. *(Josh slowly stands up and faces Mr. Sykes.)*

JOSH. She's my daughter. I think I can talk to her when I choose.

MR. SYKES. That's not what I meant.

JOSH. What ideas have you been feeding her? She's not lonely. She's got no *reason* to be lonely.

MR. SYKES. She obviously feels otherwise.

JOSH. Well, she's not always right about these things. Maybe she hasn't lived long enough to know better.

MR. SYKES. I agree.

JOSH. We're a healthy family. You understand me? There's nothing wrong with us.

MARLYS. Josh. It's not his fault.

JOSH. Yes it is. She doesn't need someone telling her how fucked up she is.

MR. SYKES. That's hardly — *(Josh pushes Mr. Sykes away.)*

JOSH. Shut up! *(Christine jumps to her feet.)*

CHRISTINE. Stop it, Dad!

JOSH. You stay away from my kid. You understand me?

MR. SYKES. Mr. Hauser, I'm not the reason she's here.

JOSH. You're saying I am? Is that what you're saying? Think again.

MARLYS. Come here, Josh. *(Dr. Grey returns, having heard the ruckus.)*

JOSH. You too! We don't need any fucking doctors! We're doing just fine without you!

CHRISTINE. Daddy! *(Marlys comes up from behind and hugs him tight, pulling him away from Mr. Sykes and Dr. Grey.)*

MARLYS. Come away, Josh. Come away from them. *(Josh breaks free.)*

JOSH. What do they know about it? What does anybody know? This is my family! It belongs to me. They can't have it.

MARLYS. All right.

JOSH. They have no idea. It means something. I know what it means.

MARLYS. So tell us. *(Pause. Josh turns to look at Marlys, wavering.)*

JOSH. What?

MARLYS. Go ahead, Josh. What is it that you know? What do

you need to tell us? *(Pause. He looks at them all with uncertainty.)*

JOSH. I don't ... They think ... You can't ... I don't ... *(He slowly begins to sit on the floor, dazed. Dr. Grey runs off.)*

MARLYS. Josh? *(He lies down on his side and slowly pulls his legs up into a fetal position. He begins to hyperventilate.)*

JOSH. I'm not ... I'm ... I ... I ... *(Marlys kneels next to him on the floor.)*

MARLYS. Josh? Josh... *(Dr. Grey returns with a syringe.)*

DR. GREY. Hold him. This will calm him down. *(Marlys and Mr. Sykes hold him down while she administers the shot. Josh begins to relax.)* Let's grab that chair. We'll find a room for your husband, Mrs. Hauser. I think we need to observe him for a night. *(They put Josh into the wheelchair without much of a struggle. They begin to wheel him off.)*

MARLYS. *(To Christine.)* Just stay put, darling. Daddy will be all right. Everything will be all right. *(Dr. Grey hesitates, momentarily alone with Christine. Her voice and manner changes.)*

DR. GREY. Hello, Cathy.

CHRISTINE. My name is ... *(She pauses, realizing.)* Grandma?

DR. GREY. You look like something the cat dragged in.

CHRISTINE. They said you were dead.

DR. GREY. Sure am. Dead as a doornail. I just wanted to see you one last time.

CHRISTINE. I should have been here with you.

DR. GREY. It's all right, dear. I know what loneliness does to a soul.

CHRISTINE. It was so stupid. I'm sorry.

DR. GREY. Hang in there, Candy.

CHRISTINE. Christine.

DR. GREY. Whichever. You'll be okay.

CHRISTINE. How do you know?

DR. GREY. I don't, really. I'm just trying to make you feel better.

CHRISTINE. Will you come back?

DR. GREY. I'm afraid not, girl. Make some friends. Get away from your damn family and find someone who understands you.

CHRISTINE. I'll try. *(Dr. Grey returns to her usual voice and manner.)*

DR. GREY. Now don't wander off. I'll send an orderly to see if you need anything. *(She exits. Christine turns front.)*
CHRISTINE. Good-bye.

Postulate of Functional Indispensability

Marlys at the podium. She faces the audience.

MARLYS. So what does this mean, to introduce a "family" atmosphere into the workplace? Is such a thing even desirable? We're all familiar with the stress and strife that families can introduce into our personal lives. Do we really want these elements in our professional lives as well? *(Pause.)* Sometimes you have to look back to the beginning. What made it all worthwhile? Maybe it was your wedding. Maybe it was the birth of your first child. Maybe it was your first home. Maybe it goes back even further, back to a time when your future was affected by no more than a chance encounter. *(Crowd noises from a wedding reception fill the stage. Soft, romantic music plays in the background. Marlys pulls a champagne glass from the front of the podium. Josh enters, wearing a camera case and carrying another glass. He wears a flowery vest.)*
JOSH. Excuse me.
MARLYS. Hi.
JOSH. I just wanted to tell you how much I enjoyed that last number.
MARLYS. I didn't write it.
JOSH. But it sounded better than the original.
MARLYS. You're obviously a man of superior taste.
JOSH. My name's Josh.
MARLYS. Marlys. Official photographer, eh?
JOSH. Pays the bills. I'm really an amateur film maker.
MARLYS. And I suppose there's a role for me.
JOSH. Not that kind of film. I'm more interested in family dynamics.

MARLYS. Ah. Horror movies.

JOSH. Sounds like you might have some stories to tell.

MARLYS. I'd better not. It tends to frighten men away.

JOSH. Must be lonely.

MARLYS. Not necessarily. Some people are meant to be alone.

JOSH. And you think you're one of them?

MARLYS. Possibly. I haven't decided.

JOSH. Maybe you just haven't met the right person.

MARLYS. I see. And you're a candidate for this position?

JOSH. Hell no. I could never be happy with just one woman.

MARLYS. Ah. The harem syndrome. How attractive.

JOSH. Unless ... I haven't met the right person either.

MARLYS. Well, there's a lot of people here. Maybe we can find partners for each other.

JOSH. This sounds like a dare.

MARLYS. Maybe it is.

JOSH. And if we don't succeed?

MARLYS. We'll be stuck with each other.

JOSH. Okay. Then there's this ninety-year-old man I'd like you to meet.

MARLYS. Throwing in the towel already?

JOSH. You shouldn't have named the terms.

MARLYS. My mistake. *(Pause. They sip champagne and look around.)*

JOSH. It's all rather Felliniesque, isn't it?

MARLYS. What exactly does that mean? "Felliniesque." I've always wondered about that.

JOSH. Like a Fellini movie. You know. *(She stares at him blankly.)* You've never seen one.

MARLYS. Did any of them star Rock Hudson?

JOSH. No.

MARLYS. Then I doubt it.

JOSH. It means excessive. Fantastical. Hallucinatory.

MARLYS. This is how you see marriage?

JOSH. No. This is how I see weddings. That's an important distinction.

MARLYS. Explain.

JOSH. Well, the decision to begin a family should have nothing to do with all these other people. With tuxedos, and cake, and endless rows of Cuisinarts. It's a private decision. Between you and the one you're meant to spend eternity with.

MARLYS. Not just life? Eternity too?

JOSH. That's how I see it.

MARLYS. Scary thought.

JOSH. I mean, you look at all this stuff, and you just wonder — who are they trying to impress? It's as though they need to convince themselves.

MARLYS. Still — we're getting paid.

JOSH. Hey, I'm not complaining.

MARLYS. Sounded like it to me.

JOSH. Well, how do you feel about it?

MARLYS. I don't think this is so bad. Maybe there's a good reason to celebrate. Once upon a time, two people met. They glanced back at each other. With luck, that first look will produce generations of new creatures contributing to a brave new world.

JOSH. So that makes it all worthwhile. Future societies will look back on this couple.

MARLYS. With admiration.

JOSH. Or resentment.

MARLYS. That's part of the risk. Or don't you believe in risk?

JOSH. Not very often.

MARLYS. I think there must be a moment in every one's life when they have to decide. Do I sit back and let life pass me by? Or do I take that step? That one decision which may have countless reverberations on the ribbon of time. That one, blinding moment — of irretrievable permanence.

JOSH. Like this? *(Josh kisses her suddenly. The music stops, Josh and Marlys look at each other with new seriousness. He backs away from her as she stares at him. She turns to the audience. But can find nothing to say. She turns and faces the breakfast table as it comes into view. She takes a seat there.)*

Pause. Marlys alone at the breakfast table. Christine runs in with a cola, grabs a textbook off the table and puts a foot on one of the kitchen chairs, tying a loose shoelace. A beat after Christine enters, Josh comes on, grabs his coffee mug off the table and takes a sip. Neither Josh or Christine sits. A brief flurry of activity surrounding Marlys. Josh checks his watch.

JOSH. Come on. I'll take you to school.
MARLYS. Sit down.
CHRISTINE. Mom, I'll be late.
MARLYS. I said sit down. *(Josh and Christine reluctantly sit.)* Don't say anything. In five minutes, you'll get your chance. In the meantime, it's my turn. Because depending on your response, I may not be here when you come home tonight. *(Pause. Josh and Christine look at each other.)*

When I was a little girl, I thought that the world was a frightening place. So I looked to my family to protect and guide me. But there was no protection. There was no guidance. I accused them for a long time. But not any longer. Because I'm just the same. I've been pretending that I'm a good wife and mother. But I'm not. I don't have the slightest idea how to go about it. I never did. *(Pause.)*

So when things went wrong, as they inevitably would, I figured it was my fault. When my family began to ignore me, I blamed myself. When my husband had an affair, I blamed myself. When my child landed in the hospital, I blamed myself. Well, guess what? I've decided it's not my fault. It's *yours.* You fucked up. So you must take the responsibility. *(She turns to Christine.)*

I know you feel damaged. It's part of your culture. You'd rather mutilate yourself than have others do it to you. It's a way to take control. I understand. But it's not my way. And I don't agree with it. *(She turns to Josh.)*

And I know what's behind the things you do. You're finding ways to distract yourself — so you don't have to think about growing old. Like your own mother. I'm sympathetic. But I don't think it's a good excuse. Because other people have learned how to handle it. And you can too. *(Pause.)*

But what really disturbs me, what hurts me to my soul, is this. Neither of you has the slightest idea how much I love you. I can't help it. And I won't deny it. After all these years, I find myself with an irrefutable wealth of love for my husband and child. Oh, I've tried to make it go away. I've told myself it's just not worth it. And believe me, it's not. We're not a very good family. Maybe no family is. But if this family — *any* family — has a purpose, it must be that we're allowed to love each other. No matter what. *(Pause.)*

I'm not afraid to love you. But if you're not willing to accept it — with all its blemishes and incompetence — I'll take it away. For good. Because it's killing me to waste it. *(Pause.)*

And if I decide to stay, I'm not promising things will be easier. We're going to fight. Maybe most of the time. But I'm not gonna let you push me away. I'll be in your face — every waking, breathing minute of your short lives. And oh yes, that *is* a threat. *(Pause.)*

That's all. The question for each of you is — can you take it? *(Pause. Christine and Josh look at each other. Christine picks up the cereal box and pours cereal into her bowl. She hands it to her father. Josh hesitates, then pours cereal into his own bowl as Christine adds milk to hers. Marlys watches them both, then speaks with satisfaction.)*

Good morning.

End of Play.

PROPERTY LIST

Coffee (JOSH)
Newspaper (JOSH)
Backpack (CHRISTINE)
Cola (CHRISTINE)
Script (JOSH)
Thermos and paper cup (MEGAN)
Electric power drill (MR. SYKES)
Electric pencil sharpener and pencil (MR. SYKES)
Note (MARLYS)
Coffee cup (MEGAN)
Medical chart (DR. GREY)
Homework (CHRISTINE)
Coffee cup (MARLYS)
Sugar (CHRISTINE)
Napkin (CHRISTINE)
Butter (CHRISTINE)
Toast (MARLYS)
Cereal (MARLYS)
Film reel (MARLYS)
Scissors (MARLYS)
Purse (MARLYS)
Credit card (MARLYS)
Roses (JOSH)
Watch (JOSH)
Josh's wallet (MARLYS)
Condom (MARLYS)
Inkblots (MR. SYKES)
Marlys' wallet (MARLYS)
Photo (MARLYS)
Picnic (MARLYS, CHRISTINE)
Insect repellent (MARLYS)
Portable grill (JOSH)
Cookies (CHRISTINE)
Leash (MEGAN)
Photos (MEGAN)

Cheese (MARLYS)
Film reels (JOSH)
Coffee cups and assorted trash (MEGAN)
English muffins (MARLYS)
Newspaper (MEGAN, MR. SYKES)
Wheelchair (CHRISTINE)
Syringe (DR. GREY)
Champagne glasses (MARLYS, JOSH)
Camera case with camera (JOSH)
Textbook (CHRISTINE)
Coffee mug (JOSH)
Cereal and milk (CHRISTINE)

SOUND EFFECTS

Crowd voices
Wedding crowd noises
Romantic music